About the author: Ricky Nevsimal M.A, M.S. is a Sociologist and a Psychologist who has taught at several Chicago area colleges. He graduated from Northern Illinois University and Western Illinois University. His purpose in writing this book was to help those with Asperger's Syndrome to have better lives, to help the parents and teachers of those with Asperger's Syndrome to better help those children and to educate the public about the disorder. This booklet can serve as a reader for the Introduction to Psychology Class or the Abnormal Psychology Class. The first part of this book explains Asperger's Syndrome and the related disorders and the second part provides practical advice to parents, teachers and Aspies.

VIGNETTES: The vignettes in this book include only fictional characters.

Dedication: Tis book is dedicated to Doctor Vernon Joy who helped me when I needed some help, was my friend and who encouraged me to write.

CONTENTS

CONTENTS

FORWARD

There are lots of people with Asperger's Syndrome (A.S.) and they're often misunderstood. Some call them science geeks or just plan geeks. They often make big contributions to the world as lots of them are very intelligent. Very difficult childhoods are typical but they often have very successful careers, but trouble dating and with marriage. Some have become very famous. Misunderstanding is part of the problem. Parents, teachers, classmates and co-workers seldom know anything about their problems. All they know is those people seem strange. The author hopes that this book will help the public to better understand A.S. and hopefully that will help people with the disorder to have better lives.

WHAT IS ASPERGER'S SYNDROME AND ITS RELATED CONDITIONS

UNDERSTANDING THE DIAGNOSIS

The world is filled with people and some of them are a little different from others. People with Asperger's Syndrome (A. S.) are eccentric and a little difficult to understand. As children they know they are different but they don't understand what's wrong with them. Neither do their classmates. Often their parents and teachers don't understand them. Everyone carries d.n.a. within him and those with A.S. are genetically a little different. They communicate differently, have trouble making friends, are often intelligent, sometimes very intelligent, and they commonly have special talents. *Many of the greatest people in history likely had A.S., and without them the world we know today would be very different*. They were scientists, composers, artists and many other things. Much of the progress humanity has achieved starting with the renaissance is really the result of A.S., so even if they seem a little strange the world would be much worse off without them. No one knows where or when A.S. started, but one possibility is it originated as a genetic fault and spread from country to country. It might have been a reproductive advantage in some situations because of its association with high intelligence

There are three generally recognized autistic spectrum disorders (pervasive developmental disorders) including Autism, AS and Pervasive Developmental Disorder Not Otherwise Specified (PDD-NOS). They include social deficits, communication deficits and repetitive interests and behaviors. Of the Three Autism is the most serious and PDD-NOS the least. All three are officially considered mental illnesses. (American Psychiatric Association. (2000). Diagnostic and statistical manual of mental disorders (4th ed. text rev.). Washington: DC: Author. DOI: 10.1176/appi.books.9780890423349)

Autism is characterized by abnormal development in social interaction, communication and repetitive or narrow interests starting before age three. (DSM-IV-TR (2000) 4th ed., text rev.) It occurs in about 2 out of 1000 children and is 4 times more common in boys. Ecolalia is common (rote repetition of what others say). So is a strong desire for sameness. Imagine a small child, who doesn't like to be touched, has great difficulty communicating, prefers to play alone and can't tolerate even a small change in his environment. As a teenager he attends school but has no friends or interest in social interaction, avoids eye contact and has trouble holding a normal conversation, might have great difficulty passing classes and wants to wear the same clothes every day, listen to the same songs over and over, insists everything in his room remain in the same place and does everything every day according to the same schedule. Some people with Autism function at a high level, possibly even working at professional jobs. The prevalence of autism appears to be increasing and that is setting off a panic because it is frightening and no one knows how to protect against it. That is why theories like vaccines producing autism have become popular. Fear of autism has led almost to panic. Some parents have refused to have their children vaccinated, opening the door for the return of infectious scourges.

A.S. is a milder form of Autism, milder but still serious. *(DSM-IV-TR (2000) 4th ed., text rev.)* The prevalence is unknown but it seems to affect boys much more often than girls. There are two key differences. With AS children appear to be normal until age three and the symptoms are less serious. Imagine a child who loves to talk, especially to adults, who has an extensive vocabulary, has a tremendous interest in one topic, has difficulty getting along with other children and has a desire for sameness but less severe than that found in those with Autism. They are often bullied. Monotone voices are typical. Most are not athletic. Some people with Asperger's Disorder attain professional jobs and some have even become noted geniuses. They might display savant talents such as speaking several foreign languages, writing successful books or playing violin like a virtuoso but have learning disabilities. Some feel at home working in science because they have less contact with others. If they have a great deal of career success they are considered eccentric but acceptable. Marriage is a big challenge which requires patience and understanding from the other partner because they are hard to live with. Some are never sexually active.

PDD-NOS, is a form of Autism that presents two basic problems. *(DSM-IV-TR (2000) 4th. ed., text rev.)* People with it have trouble with social interaction and communication. They are usually not as disabled as those diagnosed with Autism, but some are very disabled. PDD-NOS, has become a category for all those people who exhibit symptoms of Autism but who don't meet all the criteria for having full blown Autism or AS. For some the symptoms they do have are very severe.

In 1944 Dr. Hans Asperger, A Pediatrician and soon to be Medical Professor at the University of Vienna published a paper describing an Autistic Disorder that has come to be called A.S. *(Asperger, 1944)* Children with A.S. were described as having a lack of empathy, little ability to form friendships, carrying on one sided conversations, showing intense interest in a topic of interest to themselves and clumsiness. He called them Little Professors because of their ability to speak at great length about a topic of interest. It's ironic that he called them little professors because lots of people with AS have become professors. High intelligence, savant mathematical talent and intense focus are advantages in academia.

Diagnosis of AS is based on behavior evaluated against six criteria. *(Gillberg, 1991)* All six must be met for a confirmed diagnosis suing the Gillberg model. 1. Severe impairment in reciprocal social interaction as defined as at least two of the following: Inability to interact with peers, lack of desire to interact with peers, lack of appreciation of social cues and emotionally and socially inappropriate behavior. 2. All absorbing narrow interest demonstrated by at least one of the following: Exclusion of all other activities, repetitive adherence and knowledge that is more rote memorization than understanding of meaning. 3. Imposition of routines and interests on self or others. 4. Speech and language problems as indicated by at least three of the following: Delayed development, superficially perfect language, formal pedantic language, odd prosody and peculiar voice characteristics and impaired understanding of meaning including misinterpretation of literal and implied meanings. 5. Non-verbal communication problems as evidenced by at least one of the following: Limited use of gestures, clumsy or gauche body language, limited facial expression, inappropriate expression and peculiar or stiff gaze.

The American Psychiatric Society has different criteria for diagnosis. (DSM-IV-TR (2000) 4th ed., text rev.) Diagnosis requires two of the following four qualitative impairments in social interaction: 1. Impairment in the use of non-verbal communication. 2. Failure to develop age appropriate peer relationships. 3. Lack of spontaneous sharing of enjoyment, interests or achievements. 4. Lack of social or emotional reciprocity. Diagnosis also requires repetitive and stereotyped patterns of behavior, interests and activities as demonstrated by at least one of the following: 1. Abnormal preoccupation with a stereotyped and restricted interest. 2. Inflexibility of routine or ritual. 3. Stereotyped and reflexive motor mannerisms. 4. Persistent preoccupation with parts of objects. Diagnosis also requires impairment in functioning besides social impairment, no delay in language development, no delay in development of self-help skills and criteria not met for diagnosis with other Pervasive Developmental Disorders or Schizophrenia.

Current research has shown brain differences in people with A.S. have differences in brain structure among subjects with A.S. It showed specific differences in brain structure, helping to prove AS is a real disorder. There was under activation in some structures and over activation in others. In short, people with A.S. think in a different way from those who are normal. They have to because their brains are wired differently. That's both good and bad. It explains why they have some problem behaviors characteristic of the disorder and it also explains why they have some special abilities. Knowing how brain structures are different might help parents and others to understand how they need to interact with Asperger's children. Under activity occurred in the prefrontal cortex involved the caudate nucleus, the anterior cingulate and the dorsolateral prefrontal cortex. The caudate nucleus is involved with multi-modal information processing and nonverbal communication. Under activity in that part of the brain accounts for the difficulty people with A.S. have in recognizing and using nonverbal communication, a characteristic disability of the disorder. It's especially detrimental when dating or interviewing for a job because it results in misunderstandings. That contributes to the general perception that people with it are odd because they don't communicate the same way others do. The anterior cingulate is important for executive function. That is making risky decisions and moral decisions, which results in poor decision making. This part of the brain helps to suppress pleasure seeking behavior so damage to this area leaves those with the disorder vulnerable to destructive pleasure seeking behaviors including drinking and gambling. The dorsolateral prefrontal cortex is critical for working memory and relationships commitment. Damage to that area could explain why those with the disorder have difficult with long term relationships. Inability to commit to relationships makes the transition into adulthood much more difficult because it often delays or prevents marriage. Delayed activity occurred in the inferior parietal lobules and in the superior parietal lobules. (Nishitani, Avakainen and Hari, 2004) The inferior parietal lobules are important for spatial perception and the superior parietal lobules are key to metal rotation. Mental rotation is the ability to imagine what unseen sides of a two or three dimensional object look like. Those two abilities help with engineering.

Physical differences in the brain prove that A.S. isn't imaginary. That's important because some parents might be inclined to think that it isn't real. If they don't face the reality of A.S. their children will have greater difficulty.

A.S. is characterized by many strange behaviors. They include long one sided conversations, lack of eye contact, lack of facial expressions, unusual posture and gestures, obsession with one or two subjects, lack of sensitivity to the feelings of others, difficulty understanding people, monotone voice and clumsiness. (Mayo Clinic, 2010) Symptoms can include uncoordinated motor activities, repetitive routines, speech problems, excellent rote memory, unusual attachment to objects, savant talents, single mindedness and flat demeanor. (Right-Diagnosis) A.S. symptoms often include speaking with a loud voice. (National Institute of Neurological Disorders and Stroke, 2010.) Tactile sensitivity is common among those with the disorder. (Blakemore, Tavassoli, Calo, Thomas, Catmur, Frith & haggard, 2006) Light sensitivity is an issue. (Your Little Professor, n.d.) A desire for sameness a monotone voice or lack of eye contact might be easiest symptoms to recognize in a work setting. It could include wanting to wear the same clothes every day or eat the same food for lunch or listen to the same song many times. Some people might want to keep the same things in the same places all the time. A child with AS might become upset if his routine is interrupted. A professor with A.S. might wear the same clothes but in different colors to every class. He might follow the same routine in every class. A monotone voice is almost a giveaway because it can't be hidden. Lack of eye contact is also easily noticed because eye contact is expected. Mike is a Chemistry Professor with many symptoms of A.S. His students think he's a bit odd because he wears blue clothes to class every day and speaks in a monotone. Mike is a creature of routine doing the same things very day at the same times and carefully keeping each thing in its own place. People in the cafeteria make fun of him because he eats the same food for lunch every day and eats at the same time. He never makes eye contact. Although his behavior is a bit strange no one thinks too much of it because he's quite successful publishing scientific articles. He lives alone just off campus, never married and doesn't date. All he seems to think about is chemistry. One thing others noticed about him was his lack of eye contact. He said some things to students which they found offended, but he didn't seem to intend to offend them.

Uncoordinated motor activities, excellent rote memorization, savant skills and speech problems might help teachers to identify students who might have A.S. A physical education teacher could readily notice an uncoordinated child playing sports. Students with excellent rote memorization ability could stand out in many classes. Some people with A.S. have savant skills such as great mathematical ability, real musical talent, ability to speak multiple foreign languages or excellent writing skills. Those skills shine out so Asperger's students are sometimes noticed for their academic prowess. Teachers couldn't help but notice speech problems. One such problem could be putting words in the wrong order. Sandra is a good example. She's an eleven year old who mostly keeps to herself and isn't interested in gym class. She has an excellent memory and gets good grades in all her classes other than gym. French is her favorite class and she is almost fluent. She likes to practice while imagining she's French. Sandra has attracted the attention of her music teacher because she plays violin so well. All though only eleven she sometimes performs in public, playing better than most adult amateurs. A great career in classical music awaits her. Without A.S. her life would be different, but maybe not better. She would have been spared some trials, but might not have been musically talented.

Parents might notice attachment to objects, flat demeanor, single mindedness, speaking with a loud voice and sensitivity to sound and light. A child with A.S. might spend time starring at or handling an inanimate object such as a large marble. A flat demeanor is common. It's lack of emotion in situations calling for emotion. Single mindedness might stand out. That is a determination to do one thing so the child's attention is not easily distracted by another. Parents could not help but notice a child speaking in a loud voice. Another striking symptom is tactile sensitivity so those with Asperger's like to wear soft shirts and no t-shirts. It shows up wen outdoors on sunny days and during photography. Disliking bright lights should be considered as a possible indicator of AS. Ken is a good example. He seems different than other five year olds. His parents have noticed but don't understand what's wrong with him. He has a fit if his mother makes him wear a t-shirt or if he can't wear a soft shirt from his wardrobe no matter the weather or the occasion. Ken sometimes holds and stares at a glass model rocket as if it admiring it at great length. He doesn't have any friends and shows little emotion. Ken speaks in a loud voice so his parents have wondered about his hearing. Janet is also an example. She's a nine year old who hates bright lights and loud sounds. She especially hates to have her picture taken with flash photography. The noise of passing planes seems to bother her more than it does others, sometimes waking her in the night. She is abnormally attached to a stuffed animal that she insists on taking everywhere with her. She cries incessantly if she is separated from it, even taking it to school despite the teasing she gets from other children.

Some people with A.S. have special talents. (Wisconsin Medical Society, 2011) A special talent could be in mathematics, computer programming, music, painting, acting, writing speaking foreign languages, engineering chess or calendar skills. Some have more than one talent.

Mathematics and computer programming are very useful talents. A talent at mathematics is especially important for those wanting careers in mathematics, engineering or science. Marsha is an example of someone who found mathematics easy. She took all the most difficult math classes her school offered. After school she graduated from a university with a Ph.D. in mathematics and took a job teaching at a major university. Through the years she published several articles about mathematics and helped solve a major technical problem for the space program. Finally she was considered for Nobel Prize. Math was her life. She never married, but she had her career. Her students didn't really like her, but they learned a lot from her. She was department chair the last two years of her career. Now she is retired. Computer programming is a very useful talent. Little can be accomplished without it. Tom is an example of someone with a talent in computer programming. He always liked computers. He played games on his until he was old enough to use the internet. Basic was the first computer language Tom learned. After that he learned Assembler, C and Fortran. He got a degree in Computer Science and started an excellent career writing programs for an engineering firm. His programs helped engineers solve difficult scientific problems. Eventually he got an M.S. and became the head of the computer department where he worked. One of the reasons he liked working with computers was because it was easier than working with people. Today he's helping to develop a new computer language to improve satellite communications. Tom continues to use the internet with all his free time because he has nothing else to do. He can communicate with others on the internet but not well in person.

Lots of people with AS have musical or artistic talent. Clare is an example of someone with A.S. who has musical talent. She always loved music from the time she learned to play a recorder in second grade. She started to learn the clarinet in sixth grade and became a piano virtuoso by nineteen. It was clear that her career would be in music. She played in a major orchestra and recorded songs on her own. Most people she knows are musicians because she doesn't know many people outside of work. When other girls were going on dates she was playing piano. Music comforts her whenever she needs it. Clare married but it didn't work out because she could never get along with her husband. They couldn't communicate well and she was inflexible about many things. She played at her own wedding reception and her end of marriage party. Raphael is an example of someone with artistic talent. He learned to draw during art class in middle school. He started painting in high school and studied art at a university. Rafael spent lots of hours walking through art galleries and staring at paintings. He became expert at copying the works of the masters and developed a love for surrealism. The struggle was tough for the first five years after completing his degree while working at a store and painting was difficult. His work was eventually discovered. Years later he had painted many very good paintings and become a recognized expert. He managed an art gallery and eventually owned one. His employees and customers thought of him as an eccentric artist who had a somewhat hostile personality. The wine he drank was a cover for what was really going on inside of him. The pain he felt from his childhood coping with A.S. shows through in his work. His paintings are always of only one person, never human interaction. He never painted children because they remind him of the suffering he went through.

Some people with A.S. have a talent for acting or writing. It's difficult for them because they have to learn to use non-verbal communication and they have difficulty with voice. It helps that they can memorize a large number of lines. Those with acting ability can play a part because they take on the personality of whoever they are playing. Karanda is an example. She always loved acting. She started acting when she tried out for a high school play. Afterwards she thought she could never get enough of it. She got a degree in acting and started working in Community Theater while also working as a waitress. Before long she was discovered and got a part in a Broadway play. A few years later she started working in Hollywood. She was known as an excellent actress but unlike the others she didn't make the covers of the gossip papers because she avoided the starlet life style. She showed the world who it wanted to see but didn't want to show who she was. She feels insecure because others have always rejected her. The ability to be a great writer can come with A.S. Some great ones had it. Someone with AS must learn how to organize thoughts and use non-verbal communication to become a good writer. Non-verbal communication is important because characters in a story need to use it. Karl had trouble learning how to read. He started to read lots of books because his teacher and parents insisted he do so. Soon he loved to read. He wrote his first book when he was fourteen. It was a science fiction novel about space men that landed in the football field of his high school and fled into the sky taking all the school's cheerleaders with them. He got a degree in English and started writing while working as a high school teacher. Karl dated a lot, but he couldn't make a relationship work. After becoming experienced with failed relationships he became a big success writing books about characters who failed at romance. His work as a teacher was difficult because he had trouble getting along.

Some people with A.S. have a special talent for foreign languages. Maria is an example. She suffered from A.S. and became an expert in several languages. She grew up in an immigrant family that spoke Spanish at home so Spanish was her first language. Before long she started to learn English so she would be ready for school. In middle school Maria was introduced to French. She learned Italian, Portuguese and German while getting a degree. Soon she was working as a professional translator and learning a new language every year. She got a good job as a translator working for the government and was recognized as a foreign language expert. Speaking foreign languages helped her to meet people because they assumed her communication problems were due to cultural differences. The most interesting thing she could do was talk to four people in different languages at the same time.

Some people with AS have a talent for engineering, a different talent than mathematics. ***They can imagine what objects look like in second and third dimensions and even imagine them moving.*** That greatly helps them to design machinery. Bart always liked to draw so he considered becoming a draftsman. He became a mechanical engineer instead. After getting a Master's Degree in Mechanical Engineering he went to work designing race cars for NASCAR competitions. He made a name for himself because some of his cars won. Much of his time off work was spent creating inventions to save energy while at home in his garage.

A special talent at chess or calendar skills is possible. It's related to mathematical ability and working memory. Chess is an old game and some people think it trains the mind. Kings played it thinking it would prepare them for war. Jeremy is an example of someone who loved to play chess from the time he forced learned the game at eleven years old. He played all the times. By seventeen he was a ranked player competing in major tournaments. He became world champion at age thirty. Fame followed his success so he became a celebrity sometimes appearing on T.V. His one regret about his life was that he only ever had three friends. The calendar skills talent is common among people with A.S. The calendar skill is the ability to instantly know what day of the week a date occurred or will occur on hundreds of years into the past or the future. It's not useful but it can be entertaining. Mary is an example of someone who had A.S. and the calendar skill talent. She got invited to small parties because other people wanted her to entertain. It makes her interesting to others but soon her communication problems become issues.

A small number of those with A.S. have high intelligence and multiple talents. Mathematics, engineering, writing and foreign languages are especially useful. Someone with a combination of those skills has the potential to become a great scientist or engineer. Another very useful combination of talents is acting, music, painting and writing. Someone with those talents would have a good chance of becoming a wealthy celebrity. The question is which activity to concentrate on. A.S. is associated with high intelligence and savant talents but not all people with A.S. have either. Lots of people with A.S. are intelligent but don't have special talents. Some are of normal intelligence and have talents. Others are of normal intelligence and don't have special talents. It can be difficult to recognize people with A.S> because they aren't all the same.

ASSOCIATED DISORDERS

People with A.S. often have problems with anxiety and depression. Anxiety problems can significantly reduce the quality of life. Anyone with as should be observed to determine if he has other disorders. About 80% of people with A.S. also have trouble with anxiety disorders. (Kim, Szatmari, Bryson, Streiner & Wilson, 2000) Anxiety disorders include panic disorders, social anxiety disorder, phobias, generalized anxiety disorder, obsessive compulsive disorder and post-traumatic stress disorder. Those disorders are treatable, but left untreated they can make life difficult for anyone. Depression is also a problem. It has seven symptoms. 1. Disturbance of eating resulting in gaining or losing weight. 2. Disturbance of sleep. 3. Disturbance of activity level. 4. Loss of energy. 5. Feeling tired. 6. Difficulty concentrating. 7. Feelings of guilt, helplessness and hopelessness. (Halverson, 2012) Depression symptoms add suffering to what those with AS go through. The combination of the two might go undetected in childhood.

Bipolar Disorder is much more serious and unfortunately also more common among those with A.S. There is a high rate of Bipolar Disorder the relatives of those with A.S.. (National Center for Biological Information, 2008) Mood swings are the key to Bipolar Disorder. Those afflicted swing between mania and depression. Mania can include delusions of grandeur, a high energy level, heightened sex drive, irritability and less need for sleep. Depression can include sadness, anxiety, uncontrolled crying and thoughts of suicide. (Web MD, 2005) Those with Bipolar Disorder can be dangerous because of uncontrolled emotional explosions. They don't get better without treatment.

Attention Deficit Hyperactivity Disorder and Tourette's Syndrome (Mazonne, 2012) are common among those with A.S. People with Attention Deficit Hyperactivity Disorder have trouble sitting still, paying attention and self-starting. Lots of them are emotionally sensitive and have trouble with organization. (My Asperger's Child, 2009) Those with it have trouble in school because it's difficult for them to finish assignments. Dyspraxia is a neurological disorder characterized by problems transmitting instructions in the brain for movement. People who have it are uncoordinated. One of the problems they have is writing because it's difficult for them to hold a pencil or pen. They often have difficult with Attention Deficit Disorder and short term memory. The memory problem can make it difficult to remember instructions. Tourette's Syndrome is seen among those with AS. It's characterized by repetitive facial and motor ticks. The public is ware of people with Tourette's yelling out inappropriate comments but most people with Tourette's don't do that.

Alcoholism might be more common among those with A.S. *They suffer from anxiety and they might use alcohol to self-medicate.* That happens to a lot of people with anxiety but who don't have AS. Alcohol is a drug that depresses the central nervous system so it has a calming effect that comforts anxiety sufferers. That same effect can make depression worse. Unfortunately society offers few alternatives for relief of significant anxiety. There are two problems from self-medicating with alcohol. In the short run alcohol can be very dangerous because it slows motor reactions and impairs judgment. That's why it's a bad idea to drink and drive. It makes people more vulnerable.

American Psychiatric Association. (2000). *Diagnostic and statistical manual of mental disorders* (4th ed. text rev.), Washington: DC: Author. DOI: 10.1176/appibooks.9780890423349.

Blakemore, S. J., Tavassoli, T., Calo, S., Thomas, R. M., Catmur, C., Frith, U. and Haggard, P. (2006), Tactile sensitivity in Asperger Syndrome. *Brain Cognition*, 61(1): 5-13. DOI: 10.106/j.bandc.2006.02002.

Gillberg, C. (1991). *Clinical and neurobiological aspects of Asperger's Syndrome in six families studied*. In Autism and Asperger's Syndrome, (ed. U. Frith). Cambridge: Cambridge University Press. DOI: 1177/1362361302006003006.

Kim, J.A., Szatmari, P., Bryson, S.E., Streiner, D.L. and Wilson, F.J. (2000). The Prevalence of Anxiety and Mood Problems With Autism and Asperger Syndrome, *Autism*, 4(2): 117-132. DOI: 10.1177/136236130000400002002.

Mazonne, I., Ruta, L. & Reale, L., 2012. Psychiatric comorbidities in Asperger syndrome and high functioning autism : Diagnostic challenges. *Annals of General Psychiatry*, 11:16, DOI: 10.1186/1744-859X-11-16. DOI: 10.1186/1744-859X-11-16.

Nishitani, N. and Avaikainen, R. H. (2004). Abnormal imitation-related cortical activation sequences in Asperger's Syndrome. *Annals of Neurology*. V. 55, 558-562. DOI: 10.1002/ana.20031.

My Aspergers Child. (2009). Retrieved From http://www.myaspergerschild.com/2009/06/aspergers?.

National Institute of Biological Information. (2008). Retrieved From http://www.ncbi.nlm.nib.gov/pmc.articles/PMC?.

National Institute of Neurological Disorders and Stroke. (2010). Retrieved From http://www.nind.nih.gov/disorders/asperger.

Right Diagnosis. (2012). Retrieved From http://www.right-diagnosis.com'a'asperger-syndrome/symptoms.

Web Md. (2012). Retrieved From http://www.webmd.com/bipolar-disorder/default.

Wisconsin Medical Society. (2011). Retrieved From http://www.wisconsinmedicalsociety.org/savant.../frewuently_asked_questions.

Your Little Professor. (n.d.). Retrieved From http:// www.yourlittleprofesssor.com/noises.

ANXIETY

ANXIETY IS A REAL PROBLEM

Those with A. S., their parents and their teachers need to know about anxiety because it's one of the main problems associated with A.S. ***People with A.S. often, but not always suffer from severe anxiety which typically starts suddenly around adolescence with the force of an explosion, but diminishes over time.*** At first it's overwhelming and mysterious, making life very difficult, but it eventually becomes more manageable. A young person with A.S. likely won't understand why he feels so much anxiety or what to do about it. All he will know is he feels terrible and he's different from others. Someone with severe anxiety might have great difficulty explaining how he feels to others. It might best be described as chemically induced fear. The situation is made worse if parents and teachers tell a young person it's all in his head. Anxiety is a very real problem and it's not something an afflicted person can simply chose not to feel. It's every bit as involuntary as diabetes and heart disease. Understanding is called for and parents and teachers should familiarize themselves with the problem of anxiety. The more they know the more they will be able to help. People with A.S. can help themselves, but only if they understand their problems. A.S. is complex so expert advice can be very important. In a real sense knowledge is power.

Left uncontrolled anxiety can ruin lives and become almost unlivable. Students might be unable to attend school or if they do they might be unable to participate in extracurricular activities. Anxiety might make it difficult for them to sleep and study. Careers can easily be ruined because anxiety can prevent people from working or if they are able to work it can reduce their performance. That's why certain careers including medicine, law enforcement and military service are not suitable for those with A.S. who suffer from anxiety. Alcohol is part of the problem for people with A.S. because they seem to be sensitive to alcohol and at the same time are tempted to use it to self-medicate against anxiety. A young person with A.S. who could be heading for a great career as a scientist might be lost to the world because he suffers from overpowering anxiety which drives him to drink. At first he just drinks a little but over time it gradually increases until he had five or six drinks every day. Eventually he drinks two or three times every day and enough each time to feel a little drunk. After a long time drinking he becomes addicted. Anxiety can be so bad that those afflicted no longer want to live so along with alcoholism anxiety can be a motive for suicide.

Those with A.S. who have anxiety need to learn to control the anxiety they feel but they will never be free of it. With learning and practice and perhaps with medication anxiety can be limited, but not completely eliminated. Someone with anxiety management training can function very normally attending school and working and they can remain almost free of anxiety distress. The problem is they can't really be completely free of anxiety all of the time. Even with the best training anxiety will creep into their lives from time to time. When that happens, it will fell like an old enemy has returned and needs to be vanquished yet again. The fight will have to start all over. Most episodes will be mild and brief but once in a great while there will be a more severe and perhaps longer lasting one.

Anxiety is an instinct that helped primitive people to survive the dangers they faced, ignorant and basically unarmed in a world filled with danger. They didn't have much but they did have instincts to supplement their intelligence and working in groups. Instincts were critical for survival. When faced with danger the alarm signal went off causing the body to rev for action, either fight or flight. Attention focused, muscles tightened and adrenalin poured into the system increasing strength and heart rate. People were made ready to run from dinosaurs or fight each other. Imagine a mother seeing a big snake approach her young child. Without thinking her body prepares for flight. She grabs the child and runs away from the snake. Or imagine a hunter coming across a lion while hunting for small game. Without thinking he thrusts his spear into the lion time and again until it falls dead. If it weren't for instinct the child, the hunter and maybe the mother would have been killed. When the danger passed people relaxed as they returned to a normal state of arousal. They were able to live normally until another dangerous event occurred. *Anxiety was a friend that protected them*. Without anxiety humanity would have died off long ago. It was a gift from God.

Modern people seldom encounter poisonous snakes or hungry dinosaurs and most never go into battle against other people but they face different dangers. Driving is dangerous because if a driver made a mistake he could get killed and even worse if another driver made a mistake he could kill lots of people which means people aren't in control of what could happen to them. That feeling of not being in control of something dangerous is terrible for some people. It is the same when riding on a plane. If the pilot makes a mistake everyone on board will die and there was nothing anyone could do about it. As difficult as it is to be in charge of one's own destiny it was much more difficult to trust others with one's life. Taking an exam is a dangerous situation. If a student fails his dreams for the future could vanish like a puff of smoke. Public speaking is difficult for some people because they were afraid of being embarrassed. Jobs can be stressful because people are required to do difficult things and they are afraid of being fired if they don't do them well. *The modern world has lots of danger but not usually of the life or death type*.

The instinct of anxiety was made for primitive people, not modern ones and as the demands of life changed anxiety become a foe instead of a friend. Instead of a survival mechanism it became a ticking time bomb carried within each of us ready to go off without warning. In some people it went off when there was no real danger and others weren't able to relax afterwards so they remained anxious after the danger had passed. Those were the people with anxiety disorders, anxiety that wasn't completely normal and that hurt them. Treatment logically focused on two things; first preventing the danger alarm from going off when there was no need for it and second helping people return to normal after the danger passed. The big problem preventing false alarms was figuring out why the alarm went off. *Lots of people experienced intense anxiety when there was no obvious danger and they didn't know where they anxiety was coming from*. That led Psychologists to probe the unconscious mind for things that could be causing it.

Psychologists identified trait anxiety. ***Some people seemed to be vulnerable to anxiety as a result of genetics.*** Anxiety disorders occurred much more commonly in some families than in others. (Skre, Anstad, Torgerson, Lygren & Kruglen, 2007) Researchers hypothesized that a shortage of the chemical serotonin was involved. (Schinka, Busch & Robichaux-Keene, 2004) Perhaps some people were born with a predisposition to under produce serotonin and that could account for anxiety running in some families. Trait anxiety didn't explain all anxiety problems because some people with anxiety disorders came from families where no one else had those problems and sometimes having gone through a terrifying experience seemed to cause anxiety. Under production of serotonin provided a clue but it clearly wasn't the whole answer. Those people with a bad gene needed help to control anxiety so it wouldn't hurt them. That was much of the impetus for developing anti-anxiety medication. If their problem was genetics it would have to treated chemically, counseling wouldn't help. It would also be critically important for them to avoid high stress situations. For example, someone bothered by driving should try to avoid driving, especially in heavy traffic.

Current stressful events were also investigated as a cause of anxiety. ***Someone might experience anxiety because he was going through a divorce or because he lost his job, a family member died or was running out of money.*** Lots of people experience anxiety because of things happening to them at present. In that case treatment focuses on developing alternatives for coping with the present situation so the patient doesn't feel that his life is spinning out of control. That could include marriage counseling or preparation for divorce. It could also include helping the patient to find a new job or maybe even a new career. Counseling in that situation would also include helping the patient to understand what was happening, to understand lots of other people already went through the same situation and helping the patient to make good life choices. Using a relaxation technique is taught to those who need it. Medication might also be appropriate for a short time.

The damage from stress seems to accumulate. (Carrion, Weems, Reiss & 2007) Having lived through a traumatic event, even many years before can leave a patient vulnerable to new stress. That is what often happens when people survive war experiences, rape or child abuse. Those people know why they have anxiety but it's difficult for them to control how they feel. Anything that reminds them of what happened can set them off, even sounds, smells and the weather. (Boutan, Mineka & Barlo, 2001) Imagine a woman who was raped by a man with a mustache becoming very upset five years after when another man with a mustache knocks on her door or imagine a man who was a prisoner of war becoming overcome with anxiety when he encounters someone dressed in a uniform similar to that worn by the guards who tortured him. ***Typically those who have been traumatized by past events have trouble coping with minimal stresses in the present.*** An excellent example is a marine who handled himself well in combat but in civilian life he isn't able to cope. Maybe one way to think of what he goes through is everyone has only a certain amount of stress she can take in in his life. Once he has used that up he can't take anymore. As a result he is greatly stressed by small things that don't much bother others. Fortunately, the situation is more complex so with treatment that former marine probably could stand considerably more stress. Without it he might have great difficulty through life.

Sometimes the cause of anxiety is unknown. In those causes Psychologists often look to the unconscious. Freud thought everything you think, feel, do or experience is remembered on some level, even if only in the unconscious. (Freud, 1915) Perhaps something frightening happened to the patient in the past and it's remembered unconsciously but the patient isn't consciously aware of it. Psychologists often suspect abuse but it could have been a different event. In that case the cure might be counseling to help the patient uncover what happened and then deal with it. Critics say that is where psychology approaches witchcraft. By probing for an event that never occurred in the past a Psychologist could cause a false memory to form. Someone who was never abused might suddenly remember being abused and that could damage relationships with parents and others and possibly lead to violence. *A Psychologist must be especially careful when looking into the unconscious to avoid disaster for the patient.* If an event is uncovered it will undoubtedly release powerful emotions that the patient will need help dealing with. On one level it could be a relief because it would provide an explanation for the anxiety so it could be better treated and it might also explain other things that happened to the patient. For example a patient who was sexually abused might have developed a fear of sexuality that could have prevented marriage. Abuse might also have led a child to distrust adults. Having been lost in a shopping center could have caused a fear of large buildings. A near drowning experience could have caused a fear of water.

Lifestyle can contribute to anxiety. Understanding that requires understanding serotonin. Serotonin is produced from l-tryptophan which is very high in saturated fat. (Bader, 2003) Eating a diet very low in saturated fat could result in a shortage of serotonin. Females produce less serotonin than males do. (Nishazawa, Bonkelfat, Young, Leyton, Mzengeza, Montigy, Blier, & Diksic, M., 1997) Exercise seems to increases production of serotonin (Salmon, 2001) so lack of exercise might result in a shortage. Think of a teenage girl trying to be very thin, maybe anorexic and eating a vegan diet with very little saturated fat. She might suddenly start to have anxiety and not have any idea why. Think of someone who works long hours and doesn't exercise. He could experience serious anxiety. *Sometimes all that's needed to defeat anxiety is eat normal food, get enough sleep and do some exercise.* A vacation can also help.

In real life anxiety is often complex because it can have more than one cause. A patient might under produce serotonin, have lived through some traumatic events, currently be under some situation stress and might also not sleep enough or exercise. In that case treatment must be multi-faceted. A Psychologist must do what he can to offer immediate relief. That would likely include referral to a Medical Doctor for anti-anxiety medication and teaching the patient a relaxation technique. When the patient has somewhat recovered the Psychologist needs to go to work finding the causes of anxiety and dealing with them as best as possible one by one. Doing so may cause some temporary setbacks as the patient might go through some episodes of sudden intense anxiety because of what he learns in counseling. It might seem to the patient that he's not getting better but in fact he is. IF he has lots of problems it might take some time to fully recover. *Unfortunately psychology can be like that, not much happens overnight, especially with patients who have more serious problems like post-traumatic stress disorder.*

THE BASICS

People learn in lots of ways and anxiety can be learned just like anything else can be which is good because it means anxiety can be unlearned, but of course a genetic problem causing under production of serotonin can't be. People learn in simple and complex ways and no one can understand how anxiety develops or can be defeated without understanding the process of learning. *Learning can occur through classical conditioning, operant conditioning and imitation.* What they have in common is associating one thing with another. For example with classical conditioning someone might learn to associate peanut butter with choking. A four year old might choke badly while eating a very thick peanut butter sandwich. As a result he might start to gag whenever he smells peanut butter. An example of learning through operant conditioning is associating country music with good grades. A student taking an easy class might listen to country music the night before an exam and get an "a". Delighted with the grade he might prepare that way for all of his exams from then on. An example of learning by imitation is a child watching a movie in which another child is attacked by a horde of spiders while a song plays. He can learn by association from identifying with the other child. A week after when he hears that same song he might feel suddenly afraid. Once someone learns something by association he can unlearn it. The four year old afraid of peanut butter might be exposed to peanut butter several times without choking and that would extinct his fear. The "a" student might prepare the same way for four exams and fail all of them because he's taking a class too difficult for him. After failing four exams he might conclude his preparation method didn't work and stop doing it. The child afraid of spiders might see another movie about friendly spiders and stop being afraid of them. The point is there's hope. We know how people learn to be afraid so we can teach them not to be afraid, to a certain extent.

Classical conditioning was discovered by Ivan Pavlov. (Pavlov, 1927) He did what became a Noble Prize winning experiment teaching dogs to salivate. Dogs naturally salivate when they are preparing to eat. He presented some dogs with meat powder (unconditioned stimulus) and they salivated (unconditioned response). No learning was involved because they dogs acted out of instinct. After that he rang a bell (conditioned stimulus) while presenting meat powder and the dogs salivated. After several trials he rang a bell but didn't present meat powder. The dogs salivated anyway. Salivating to the sound of a bell wasn't a result of instinct because it wasn't something dogs normally did so it had to have been learned. The dogs learned to associate the sound of a bell with the presentation of meat powder so when they heard a bell ring they began to salivate. Pavlov then rang the bell several times without presenting meat powder and the dogs learned to unassociated the bell with meat powder so they stopped salivating when they heard a bell. *Pavlov showed that dogs could learn and unlearn by association which was critically important to understanding phobias.* People learn like dogs do and that explains most phobias. They are the result of inappropriate learning and they can be unlearned freeing sufferers from anxiety. A woman raped by a man with a mustache might develop a terrible fear of any man with a mustache. She might learn not to be afraid of mustaches by interacting with several nice men who have mustaches.

Classical conditioning is learning to associate an action with a consequence, be it a reward or a punishment. Thorndike's law made clear how operant conditioning worked. (Thorndike, 1911) *One adjusts his behavior to gain rewards and avoid punishments*. That is very useful for parents and teachers to know and was also helpful in organizational psychology but it is also applicable to anxiety disorders. A patient might have panic attacks when leaving home and associate leaving home with having panic attacks. Imagine a woman who suddenly becomes terrified, has difficulty breathing and experiences rapid heart rate whenever she leaves her house. That could result in agoraphobia leaving the patient home bound out of fear. Inappropriate learning might leave her unable to live a normal life. She could not have been able to hold a job or go shopping or even go to doctors' appointments. It could be horrible if her house caught fire. After the consequence is removed the behavior could eventually be unlearned. After the patient starts taking anti-anxiety medication she might be coaxed out of her home and surprised when she doesn't have a panic attack. The next day she might leave her home on her own and after a few days of leaving home she might no longer have agoraphobia.

Observational learning is learning by association through the experience of someone else. *If a child sees something happen to someone else he might identify with that other person and learn to associate the behavior of that other person with the consequence.* Imagine that watching a professional wrestler win a match by knocking down his opponent the child might knock down a younger sibling hoping to gain success and applause. That child learned to be aggressive through inappropriate learning. That child could learn not to be aggressive by being mildly punished for it. It would also help to explain to him that he is not a professional wrestler and while it might be appropriate for a professional wrestler on television to behave like that it most definitely isn't appropriate for a child to do that. Breaking the child's identification with the professional wrestler might prevent him from copying the behavior of the wrestler. It would be more difficult if a boy learned to fear thunderstorms by watching his father become afraid whenever he heard thunder. A phobia can be learned in that way. A father is by definition the primary role model for his son so it would be difficult and probably harmful to break a boy's identification with his father. It would be very helpful if the father overcame his fear and showed his son that thunderstorms were nothing to be afraid of.

It's also a good idea to become familiar with the unconscious because anxiety can hide there. Freud was credited with the discovery of the unconscious. (Freud, S., 1915) It can be thought of as a secret part of the mind because memories can hide there. They still exist but they can't normally be brought to consciousness so they can't be dealt with. A student of anxiety needs to know how the unconscious functions. Think of someone who doesn't remember anything about his fourth birthday but one day while listening to a song from that time he suddenly remembers being at a party that day. He even recalls the presents he got. Memories from that birthday must have been in his mind but for some reason who couldn't recall them until he heard the song that reminded him of that day. A terrible event could be suppressed in memory hidden in a secret part of the unconscious from where it could generate a lot of anxiety without the person being able to recall it. A Psychologist might help the patient to remember the event and then deal with it so hopefully it won't bother him anymore.

A panic attack is frightening, especially the first one someone has. The symptoms are often the same as in a heart attack, especially for a big panic attack. *It's hard to breathe, the heart races, there can be chest pain, enormous anxiety suddenly occurs, the throat closes and there's an impending fear of death*. An attack can last as long as half an hour. Lots of people have a few panic attacks in a lifetime but people with panic disorder have them often. Some have them three of four times every day. One of their problems is communicating to others how bad a panic attack really is. To make it worse an attack can occur at anytime and anywhere. An attack can occur when driving on a highway, while at work, while on a date or while asleep. It's understandable that those with panic disorder (P.D.) live in fear of having attacks. If untreated there's a risk of suicide (Johnson, Wessman & Klerman, 1990). At least in that sense P.D. can kill.

The suffocation false alarm hypothesis provides an insight into what a panic attack really is but genetics do matter. (Klein, 1993) According to that hypothesis the brain has a suffocation alarm mechanism that helped to keep primitive people alive. A shortage of cave meant primitive people had to sleep in caves. The cave entrances sometimes collapsed causing a buildup of carbon dioxide which killed the people sleeping inside. A suffocation alarm developed to protect people. When the alarm senses suffocation is imminent it sends a signal to alert the person of danger. That signal is a panic attack. It hurts modern people but it helped primitive people. *In some people the suffocation alarm goes off when there's no danger.* That is P.D. For some reason in those people the alarm is overly sensitive. That explains much of the research. P.D. is more common among smokers (Isensee, Withchen, Stein, Hotler, & Diplstat, 2003) probably because they have lower blood oxygen content. Aerobic exercise helps protect against panic attacks, likely because it increases the blood oxygen level. (Strohle, 2005) Breathing carbon dioxide lowers the level of oxygen in the blood and increases the risk of panic attacks. (Papp, Martinez, Klein, Coplan, Norman, Cole, De Jesus, Ross, Goestz, & Gorman, 1997) One of the big mysteries of panic disorder is the role of caffeine. For an unknown reason caffeine greatly aggravates panic disorder. (Charney, Heninger, & Jatlow, 1985) Stress often leads to anxiety and anxiety can trigger panic attacks. That's a very big problem because fear of having a panic attack can cause a panic attack. A shortage of oxygen might sensitize the suffocation alarm. People who survive a near suffocation experience have a much higher rate of P.D. (Bauwer & Stein, 1985) Contrary to this theory genetics play a role. (Crowe, Noyes, Paulus, & Slyman, 1983)

P.D. can be treated. *A big part of the treatment is lifestyle change.* Someone with panic disorder who smokes must stop. If he consumes caffeine he must stop. It's important to do aerobic exercise for at least forty minutes plus warm up and cool down at least three times a week. Getting enough sleep should be a priority. Using a relaxation technique and avoiding stress are also keys. Medication is often required. Therapy can also help. A therapist would teach a patient with panic disorder to relax, avoid stress. He would also reassure him that he's not going crazy and listen to him talk about his problems. Selective Serotonin Reuptake Inhibitors are often prescribed.

Those with obsessive compulsive disorder (O.C.D.) feel compelled to do strange things. They can generally be placed in five categories. (Calamari, Weigartz, & Janek, 1999) Washers think they have to wash their hands countless times each day to avoid contamination. They don't like to shake hands or touch things and they live in fear of germs. Checkers have to check things like doors and windows several times every day to feel safe. They aren't sure if a door or window is really locked even though they just checked it. Doubters and sinners live in fear they will be punished if they don't do something perfectly. A sinner might think he's doomed to Hell for having committed the smallest sin. Counters and arrangers constantly count things or arrange them according to a rule. A counter must have to stop to count the windows in every building he paces. Hoarders save things compulsively. A hoarder could same string or newspapers for many years. **The public doesn't understand those with obsessive compulsive disorder, perhaps not realizing that it's a mental illness**.

The cause of O.C.D. is unknown but there are some clues. Those with the disorder have abnormal brain function (Kaplan, 2010) and that points to a possible genetic cause (Pauls, Towbin, Leckman, Zahner & Cohen, 1986) or an infectious agent (Murphy, Sajid, Soto, Shapira, Edge, Yang, Lewis, & Goodman, 2003). Serotonin plays an important role. (Pigott, & Seay, 1999) For that reason anxiety can aggravate obsessive compulsive disorder and obsessive compulsive disorder can cause anxiety. Anxiety consumes serotonin so someone suffering from anxiety is likely to run short of it. Once the brain is short of serotonin obsessive compulsive disorder begins in susceptible individuals. *In that way the disorder become a vicious cycle driving the afflicted further and further into illness until something happens to break the cycle.*

Left untreated O.C.D. can become maddening. Imagine a woman who must count every car she sees. If she lives in New York City how many cars would she have to count each day? There would be no way she could leave her apartment so work and shopping would be out of the question. She might also feel compelled to clean constantly so her apartment would look perfect. *Her life would be terrible, cut off from the world.*

O.C.D. can be treated. Treatment can include reducing exposure, cognitive therapy and medication. For a hoarder of newspapers reducing exposure could be cancelling a subscription so papers would be harder to get. Cognitive therapy is teaching a patient to think differently. Someone with a hand washing compulsion might be taught to resist the urge to wash for as long as possible and to refocus his attention on something else. Selective serotonin Reuptake Inhibitors can help reduce compulsive urges. Anxiety aggravates obsessive compulsive disorder so controlling anxiety is important. That includes avoiding stressful situations, doing aerobic exercise, getting enough sleep and using a relaxation technique. Obsessive compulsive disorder is difficult to treat so it takes times to get better. Think of it as filling a glass with water one drop at a time. *It will eventually get full and each drop along the way will help a tiny bit.*

GENERALIZED ANXIETY DISORDER

People with generalized anxiety disorder (G.A.D.) worry all of the time over nothing. Catastrophizing is the key to understanding the disorder. Catastrophizing is thinking the worst in every situation. Imagine a wife terribly upset because she thinks her husband must have died in a car crash because he is fifteen minutes late home from work or a mother preparing her son for school who worries constantly that other boys will beat him up. It's normal to worry when facing danger but those with generalized anxiety disorder worry constantly when there is no danger. Worry is their preoccupation and they don't have time for anything else. *As a result they are constantly overwhelmed by anxiety so they have trouble sleeping, trouble concentrating, trouble working and they have a host of anxiety symptoms.* So much anxiety could cause physical illness. It could strain relationships thus causing even more anxiety. Anxiety can set off a chain reaction of problems.

The cause of G.A.D. is unknown but there appears to be a genetic link (Sherrer, True, Xian, Lyons, Eisen, Goldberg, Lin, & Tsuang, 2000). *A genetic link probably effects serotonin, the most important chemical in the brain for sufferers of anxiety.* Illness and family conflict can lead to anxiety which can further reduce serotonin. Anxiety from catastrophizing reduces serotonin even more making the disorder worse. Professional intervention is usually needed, especially if the symptoms are severe.

G.A.D. can ruin someone's life. Think about a young woman with the disorder worrying all of the time. She has trouble sleeping because when she lays in bed she's tormented by thoughts of her house burning down around her, one of her children dying or her marriage ending in divorce because her husband is having an affair. She awakes several times each night so she's very tired al day every day. While preparing breakfast she constantly worried that the food she is about to serve her family is poison and they will die if they eat it. Next, she drives her children to school all the time thinking another driver we cross the center line and kill her children and her. While at home she tries to clean but it's hard because she keeps expecting a phone call from school telling her that her children have died. In the afternoon she drives to school to pick up her children but she keeps thinking a terrorist might start shooting at her from one of the houses she drives by. All evening she worries that her husband will tell her that he is dying from cancer. All she can look forward to is another sleepless night. Every day is more or less the same for her so it's understandable that she's completely over whelmed. She needs someone to help her.

Treatment can include medication, relaxation and cognitive therapy. *Benzodiazepines are often prescribed for powerful immediate relief.* That probably needs to occur before therapy can be effective. Someone with generalized anxiety disorder needs to spend time relaxing, not only to reduce anxiety symptoms but also because performing a relaxation technique focus thought on something nonthreatening. Cognitive therapy teaches patients that catastrophizing is irrational and it helps patients develop better coping skills so they feel more confident about being able to handle stressful situations. It's very important to avoid caffeine, do aerobic exercise and get sufficient sleep. The support of family and friends is important.

Social anxiety disorder (S.A.D.) is fear of being judged by others which leads to avoidance of social situations. When someone with S.A.D. is being judged by others blushing, rapid heart bet, difficulty breathing, mild going blank and stomach ache can occur. An excellent example is a young woman who wants to wear a bikini to a beach but when she gets to the beach she suddenly has trouble breathing, blushes, notices her heart racing, feels a small pain in her stomach and her mind goes blank. When a man approaches her and starts talking to her she either runs into the water or back to her car. Another example is a man arriving at a job interview shaking hands with the interviewer but feeling very nervous suddenly forgets his name. Despite repeated prompting he won't give his name because he can't. All he can do is try to change the subject. He feels sick to his stomach and has to leave the interview early. ***Social anxiety is fear of others not thinking you are good enough***. Someone with social anxiety disorder might be alright in a nonjudgmental situation, but might be shy. The fear judgment is irrational. The woman in the bikini might be beautiful and the man in the job interview might be more than qualified for the job. Fear of being judged when one really is likely to fail is not an anxiety disorder. Irrational fear is the definition of an anxiety disorder.

While not as serious as some other anxiety problems social anxiety disorder can be a big problem. It can prevent people from getting jobs, getting married, getting dates and meeting people. Imagine a young man who desperately wants to date but he can't because every time he tries to ask a woman to go out with him he feels so much anxiety that he runs away. ***If he can't get over his fear he'll never get any dates so he'll never marry and never have the family he wants***. Social anxiety disorder shouldn't be ignored.

Biology and learning can work together to explain S.A.D.. ***Genetics might play a role in causing social anxiety disorder.*** It could be thought of as extreme shyness. Irritable infants are at high risk of developing social anxiety disorder (Kagan,1989) and as infants they had higher resting heart rates (Kagan, Rezneck & Snidman, 1988)

988) so those with the disorder are probably genetically different. It's likely that neurotransmitters are involved. Operant conditioning might be involved. Perhaps the woman in the bikini was fat two years earlier and when she went to a beach, men teased her. Observational learning could explain some cases of social anxiety disorder. Perhaps the woman wasn't teased but saw another woman teased and rejected by men. Maybe the man in the job interview learned to fear that situation because he saw his father grow fearful when preparing for an interview. ***Someone afraid of being judged would likely tell himself that he wasn't good enough, further increasing his fear***.

Cognitive therapy and lifestyle therapy can help. Therapy can help the sufferer to understand that the fear is irrational and to provide reassurance. ***Increasing confidence would definitely help***. Someone with social anxiety disorder might avoid a problem by refocusing, that is thinking about something comforting while in a stressful situation. Basic anxiety treatment including adequate sleep, exercise and avoiding caffeine would also be helpful.

SPECIFIC PHOBIA

A phobia is an irrational fear. Some fears are rational. Anyone would be afraid if while flying in an airliner both pilots fell dead. That would be completely rational. In fact it would be irrational not to be afraid in that situation. Being afraid to board a perfectly good plane with two qualified pilots on board isn't rational. Imagine a child afraid of monsters, a very common phobia. He might not be able to sleep until his mother checks everywhere in his room to make sure there are no monsters hiding there or imagine a university student who can't pass a class because fear of public speaking prevents him from giving a presentation.   A child afraid of the dark, strangers or snakes is special case because those phobias are probably instinctual, that means they are irrational on one level and perhaps rational on another.

A phobia could be a serious problem or a very small problem. Firemen who are afraid of fire have a very serious problem and so do pilots who are afraid of flying. *A phobia can end a career.* On the other hand a dentist who's afraid of rats has only a small problem that he can probably live with because he's unlikely to encounter any rats. Someone with a serious phobia problem needs help to overcome it, but someone with a minor phobia problem can get by in life quite well without treatment. Some phobias fade over time so not all of them need be treated. Children seem to overcome fear of the dark on their own.

Genetics, operant conditioning, classical conditioning and observational learning can explain phobias. A predisposition for phobias might be inherited. (Kendler, Myers, Prescott & Neale, 2001) It could also result from operant conditioning. For example, an air force pilot who barely survives aerial combat might become suddenly afraid of flying. Classical conditioning causes some phobias. Think of someone who survives a bad car accident that occurs during a thunderstorm and as a result becomes very frightened whenever he's in a thunderstorm. Observational learning causes phobias. A child who watches people drown in a movie might become very afraid of water and refuse to swim. *Phobias are common because they can be acquired in multiple ways*. They can also be learned at any time. Some people develop work related phobias after working at a job for many years.

Phobias can be unlearned and basic lifestyle changes can help. *A pilot who is afraid to fly because of a combat experience might never fly again but others can be helped more easily*. No one can be anxious and relaxed at the same time.   A child afraid of dogs could be gradually exposed to dogs while relaxed in a safe environment.   During the first session he might completely relax before the therapist talks to him about dogs. In the second session he would completely relax and then watch a movie about small friendly dogs. During the third session after relaxing he would talk to the therapist about a subject he likes while the therapist holds a small friendly dog. In the fourth session the boy would relax and then hold and pet the dog. In the fifth session the therapist and the dog would go for a walk passing by several dogs. Of course as with other anxiety disorders getting enough sleep, doing some aerobic exercise and avoiding caffeine can help.

Post-traumatic stress disorder (P.T.S.D.) is the most serious of the anxiety problems. It's caused by a traumatic event such as combat, rape or other criminal attack. Anxiety can begin to take hold after surviving a terrible event. *Symptoms can include flashbacks, nightmares, emotional numbness, trouble concentrating and difficulty with relationships.* (DSM-IV-TR (2000) 4th ed., text rev.) Those with the disorder are often very anxious. A woman victimized by rape could develop the disorder as a result. She might seem upset but otherwise alright immediately after the event but she could develop problems latter. A few weeks after the crime the symptoms could start. While trying to relax at home she might experience a flashback. It could be almost as if the event was happening again and that could add more psychological trauma. She might be damaged many times as flashbacks continue to occur. One of her problems could be trouble sleeping because she might be plagued by nightmares that force her to relive the event. When told about the suffering of someone else she could be unable to feel empathy because of emotional numbing. She could experience trouble concentrating on her work. It might not be possible for her to provide details of what happened because she might be able to remember them. Relationships with family members might become conflicted.

Classical conditioning can make P.T.S.D. much worse. The woman in the example above might have associated several stimuli with the rape. Perhaps it was raining at the time, a dog was barking nearby and she heard the sound of a car horn. Latter she felt terribly afraid every time it rained but had no idea why. She became physically sick from stress whenever she heard a dog bark so she had to hide in her home unable to do many of the normal things of life. Whenever she heard a car horn her throat closed, she became sick to her stomach and threw up.

Untreated, someone with P.T.S.D. lives in a hellish world. Think of a veteran who survived repeated close combat. After returning home he remained a nervous wreck for many years. Every time he heard he heard a helicopter he freaked out, running into his home to hide. The sound of a gunshot prevented him from sleeping for two days. Unable to cope with severe anxiety and unwilling to seek treatment he turned to alcohol for relief. He became an alcoholic but anxiety continued to plague him. Unable to work he became dependent on disability payments and was forced to live in poverty. The marriage he started before going to war ended with bitter fighting. Thinking he had nothing to live for he killed himself. What started in a faraway country led to disaster in America and ruined countless lives of civilians here.

P.T.S.D. is clearly caused by a traumatic event but other factors are involved. It's more common among those who have relatives with anxiety disorders (Brewin, Andrews, & Valentine, 2000) and those who had stressful childhoods (U.S. National Library of medicine, 2012). A genetic predisposition to under produce serotonin almost certainly places some at greater risk. Anxiety seems to have a cumulative effect so those who went through difficult childhoods are at greater risk. *The combination of under production of serotonin and bad childhood experiences leaves people very vulnerable.* It would be best for people at risk to avoid stress.

Medication, lifestyle and cognitive therapy can relieve suffering. It is an anxiety disorder so anti-anxiety medication reduces its symptoms. Anti-depression medication is commonly used because lots of people with post-traumatic stress disorder are depressed. Anti-psychotic medication is sometimes prescribed, usually temporarily because some people with post-traumatic stress disorder show symptoms of psychosis, especially flashbacks. Prazosin might be used to suppress nightmares so the patient can sleep better. Difficult thought it may be for someone with post-traumatic stress disorder to sleep well it's very important. Doing some aerobic exercise and avoiding caffeine is also important. With cognitive therapy a patient first relaxes and then talks about the terrible experience he went through. That's repeated many times. The patient is also gradually exposed to those stimuli he associated with the event but in a relaxed and safe environment until he no longer fears them. (refer to the section on specific phobias in this chapter)

American Psychiatric Association (2000). *Diagnostic and Statistical Manual of Mental Disorder*, (4th ed., text rev,). Washington, D C: Author. DOI: 10.1176/appibooks.9780890423349.

Brewin, C. R., Andrews, B. and Valentine, J. D. (2000). Meta-Analysis of Risk factors for Post-Traumatic Stress Disorder in Trauma Exposed Adults. *Journal of Consulting and Clinical Psychology*, 68(5): 748-766. DOI: 10.1037/0022-006X.68.5.748.

Boutan, M., Mineka, S. & Barlo, D.H. (2001). A Contemporary Learning Theory Perspective on the Etiology of Panic Disorder. *Psychological Review*. 108, 4-32. DOI: 10.1037/0033-066X.61.1.10

Bower, C. and Stein, D.J. (1985). Association of Panic Disorder With History of Traumatic Suffocation. *American Journal of Psychiatry*. (3): 1566-1570. DOI: 10.1016/S0376-8716(03)00070-X.

Calamari, J. E., Wiegartz, P.S. and Janek, T.S. (1999). Obsessive-Compulsive Disorder Subgroups. *Behavior Research Therapy*. 37(2): 113-125. DOI: 10.1016/S0005—7967(98)000135-1.

Carrion, V.G., Weems, C.F. & Reiss, A.L., (2007). Stress Predicts Changes in Children: A pilot Longitudinal Study on Youth Stress, Posttraumatic Stress Disorder and the Hippocampus. *Pediatrics*, 119(3): 509-526. DOI: 10.1542/peds.2006-2028.

Charney, D.S., Heninger, G.R. and Jatlow, P.I. (1985). Increased Axiogenic Effects of Caffeine in Panic Disorder. *Archives of General Psychiatry*, 42(3): 233-243. DOI: 10.1001/arcpsych.1985.01790260027003.

Crowe, R.R., Noyes, R.N., Paulus, D.L. and Slyman, D. A Family Study of Panic Disorder (1983*). Archives of General Psychiatry*, 40(10): 1065-1069. DOI: 10.1001/archpsych.1983.0179000027004.

Freud, S., (1915 ed). Das Unbewusste, *Int. Z. Psychoanalasis*, 3(4): 189-203 and 257-369, translated 1925 by Baines, C.M., Repression.

Inesee, B., Witchen, H., Stein., M. Hofler., M. and Diplstat, R.L. (2003). Smoking Increases the Risk of Panic. *Archives of General Psychiatry*, 60(7): 692-700. DOI: 10.1001/arcpsych.60.7.692.

Johnson, J., Wessman, M. M. and Klerman, G. (1990). Panic Disorder Comorbidity and Suicide Attempts. *Archives of General Psychiatry*, 47(9): 805-808. DOI: 10.1001/archpsych.1990.01810210013002.

Kagan, J. (1989). Tempermental Contributions to Social Behavior. *American Psychologist*, 44: 668-674. DOI: 10.1037/0003/066X.44.4.668.

Kagan, J., Rezneck, J.S. and Snidman, N. (1988). Biological Basis of Childhood Shyness. *Science*, 240: 167-171. Retrieved From http://links.jstor.org/sici?=003-8075%29880408&293%3A240%3A4849%3C167%3ABBOC5%3E2.0.CO%3B2-1.

Kendler, K., Myers, J., Prescott, C. A. and Neale, M. C. (2001). The Genetic Epidemiology of Irrational fears and Phobias in Men. *Archive of General Psychology*, 58(3): 257-265. DOI: 10.1001/archpsych.58.3.257.

Klein, D. (1993). False Suffocation Alarm, Spontaneous Panics and related Conditions. *Archives of General Psychiatry*, 50(40): 306-317. DOI: 10.1001/archpsych.1993.0182160076009.

Murphy, T. K., Sajid, M., Soto, O., Shapanira, N., Eagle, P., Young, M., Lewis, M. H. and Goodman, W. K. (2003). Detecting Pediatric Autoimmune Neuropsychiatric Disorders Associated With Streptococcus in Children With Obsessive-Compulsive Disorder and Tourette's. *Biological Psychiatry*, 55(1): 61-68. DOI: 10.1016/S0006-3223(3)00704-2.

Nishazawa, S., Benkelfat, C., Young, S.N., Leython, M., Menzengeza, S., Montigy, C., Blier, P. and Diksic, M. (1997). Differences Between male and Female Rate of Serotonin Synthesis in Human Beings. *Nat Acad Sci USA.*, 94(10): 5808-53313.

Papp, L.A. Martinez, J.M., Klein D., Coplan, J.D., Norman, R.G., Cole, R., de Jesus, M.J., Ross, D., Goetz, R. and Gorman, J. M. (1997). Respiratory Psychophysiology of Panic Disorder. *American Journal of Psychiatry*, 154(11): 1557-1565.

Pauls, D.L., Towbin, K.E., Leckman, J.F., Zahner, G.E.P. and Cohen, D.J. (1986). The inheritance of Gilles de la Tourette's Syndrome and Obsessive-Compulsive Disorder. *Archives of General Psychiatry*, 43(12): 1180-1182. DOI: 10.1056/NEJM198610163.5.604.

Pavlov, I., (1927). *Conditioned Reflexes: An Investigation of the Physiological Activity of the Cerebral Cortex*. G. V. Anrep (ed. and tr.). London: Oxford University Press.

Pigott, T.A. and Seay, S.M. (1999). A review of the Efficacy of Serotonin Reuptake Inhibitors in Obsessive-Compulsive Disorders. *Journal of Clinical Psychiatry*, 60(2): 101-106. DOI: 10.4088/JCP.v60n0206.

Salmon, P. (2001). Effects of Physical Exercise on Anxiety, Depression and Sensitivity to Stress: A Unifying Theory. *Clinical Psychology Review*, 21(1): 33-61. DOI: 10.1016/S0272-7358(99)00032-X.

Schinka, J.A., Busch, R. M., Robichaux-Keene, N. (2004). A Meta-Analysis of the Association Between the Serotonin Transporter Gene Polymorphism (5-HTTLPR) and Trait Anxiety. *Molecular Psychiatry*, (9) 197-202. DOI: 10.1038/sj.mp4001405.

Sherrer, J.F., True, W.R., Xian, H., Lyons, M.H., Eisen, S.A., Goldberg, J., Lin, N. and Tsuang, M.T. (2000). Evidence of Genetic Influences Common and Specific to Symptoms of Generalized Anxiety and Panic. *Journal of Affective Disorders*, 57(1-3): 25-35. DOI: 10.1016/S0165-0327(99)00031-2.

Skre, Anstad, Torgerson, Lygren & Kruglen, (2007). A twin study of DSM-III-R anxiety disorders. *Acta Psychiatrica Scandinavaca*, 88(2): 85-92, DOI: 10.1111/j1600-0447.1993.tb03419.x.

Strohle, A., et al. (2005). The Acute Antipanic Activity of Aerobic Exercise. *The American Journal of Psychiatry*, 162: 2376-2378. DOI: 10.1176/appi.ajp.162.12.2376.

Thorndike, E. L. (1911). *Animal Intelligence.* MacMIllan, New York, 244.

DEPRESSION

DEPRESSION IS A BIG PROBLEM

Depression affects those with Asperger's Syndrome. They seem to have a very high rate of depression and depression hurts everyone it touches. It's understandable that someone with Asperger's Syndrome would feel depressed. Life is difficult for everyone, but more so for them because they must learn to accept and find joy with lives of relative social isolation. Imagine a child with Asperger's Syndrome as an athlete climbing a hill. Other children run up the hill the hill with no problem. Those with Asperger's Syndrome climb the same hill but the disorder is like carrying a ten pound weight so it's a significant disadvantage. Anxiety adds another ten pound weight and so does depression. That means some children must climb with an extra thirty pound burden. Some might make it to the top but lots won't. *Parents of Asperger's Syndrome children and those with Asperger's Syndrome themselves must be alert to the start of depression so action can be taken to prevent it.* That's a bit challenging because depression starts gradually so it sneaks up on people. The very beginning might go unnoticed. Think about a ten year old boy who becomes depressed. He feels a little down when it starts but is able to do all of his normal activities. After a while he becomes more depressed so he doesn't want to do his homework or even go to school. Soon he doesn't want to spend time with his friends. He has no energy and doesn't like himself. He talks about his failures and others being so much better than he is. That really is the key to understanding depression. *Depressed people have low self-esteem so they think they have little control over their own lives.* Depression leads to his grades falling, which gives him more reason to be depressed. Little things that bring joy to other boys don't mean anything to him.

Untreated depression is dangerous because it can lead to other problems. *Someone who is depressed might use alcohol in an attempt to feel better.* That is he might self-medicate using alcohol instead of an anti-depressant. It can also lead to suicide because a depressed person might see no reason to continue living. A marriage could be ruined by depression. Even if those things don't happen depression robs people of the joy that everyone should experience and it leaves lots of people unproductive.

Depression can be treated. Some kinds of medication and aerobic exercise might help. Cognitive therapy can be useful. A big part of treating depression is teaching the patient to take control of his own life. As that happens he gains confidence and his self-esteem increases. Nothing banishes depression like success. Imagine a fifteen year old girl who has been experiencing mild depression. She wins an important music contest at school and a boy she likes asks her to a dance. Suddenly she's no longer depressed. Joy has replaced sadness because she now feels her life is getting better. Think of a depressed unemployed person who sits around all day thinking nothing good will ever happen for him. One day he gets a new job and suddenly his outlook brightens. His problems seem to get a lot smaller and he has new hope. *A positive change in circumstance can be powerful medicine for depression.* Someone with Asperger's Syndrome could benefit greatly from making one good friend. It would provide affirmation of self-worth.

Martin Seligman (1967) demonstrated the concept of learned helplessness. He showed that if dogs were conditioned to believe they could control what happened to them they would act to avoid discomfort in the future but dogs who were conditioned to believe they couldn't control what happened to them took no action to avoid future suffering. In that well known study dogs were placed in a cage and subjected to electric shock that they could end the shock by pushing a lever. When latter placed in a divided box, one half of which administered an electric shock, easily jumped from the side that gave a shock to the side that didn't. They took action to avoid suffering, apparently because they were confident in their ability to affect what happened to them. A second group of dogs were placed in a cage and given an electric shock that they couldn't turn off. When latter placed in the same divided box as the other dogs they made no effort to escape the electric shock. Apparently they learned that they couldn't do anything to avoid suffering in the first situation, so they took no action in the second. The dogs in the second group exhibited learned helplessness, a condition common in depressed people. Instead of taking action to improve their lives lots of depressed people simply accept whatever bad things happen to them. They go through life suffering even when they could easily avoid doing so. Those people around them don't understand them because they fail to comprehend the power of previous conditioned that led them to develop learned helplessness. In a sense they are prisoners of their past.

People with Asperger's Syndrome live in a learned helplessness situation. Almost everyone seems to feel a need to be connected to others. People are apparently not intended to live alone. Those with Asperger's Syndrome have great difficulty establishing connections to others so they feel isolated, not a natural state for people. They often learn in childhood that there's little or nothing they can do to establish social relationships. They try to make friends and become popular over and over until they become convinced there's nothing they can do. ***When that happens they exhibit learned helplessness. They give up seeking friendship and they feel depressed.*** Bullying can contribute to depression. Imagine a seven year old boy who is bullied every day at school. He complains to his teachers who fail to stop it. Latter he complains to his parents and they also fail to stop it. Eventually he accepts the abuse concluding being bullied is part of his life and put up with other boys hurting him. He might make no effort to defend himself having concluded it doesn't work. That would invite even more bullying. Another example is a child who studies hard but fails. He might conclude that there's nothing he can do to succeed so he might give up trying. If that happens he will definitely fail.

A child with learned helplessness needs to learn that he can affect his own life. Social acceptance is very important for an isolated child. A child with Asperger's Syndrome might make a friend, especially if a parent or a teacher helps. Friendship with another child who has Asperger's Syndrome could happen. A good relationship with a sibling could be a substitute. If social acceptance isn't possible other success becomes even more important. Possibly academic or musical success could be a partial substitute. Academic or other success could also help a child to make friends.

WORDS CAN HURT

Words can hurt people because they can cause depression. Aaron Beck postulated that negative thoughts could cause depression. (Beck, 1967) According to his idea self-esteem is critical for healthy psychological adjustment and low self-esteem can cause depression. Negative thoughts can cause low self-esteem. Imagine a university student who has trouble getting a date. Each time he tries and fails he might say to himself women will never be attracted to me because I'm ugly. Eventually he'll believe that he's ugly. When that happens he will have low self-esteem and might become depressed. *The words he said to himself hurt*. He didn't set out to hurt himself, it just happened. What someone says to himself can hurt even if it's counterfactual. Think of an Olympic runner. He's trained hard all of his life for one race. After several years he qualified for the team and travelled to the games. Everyone expected him to win the gold medal but he only placed fourth. Instead of spending the rest of his life proud that he was the fourth fastest runner in the world he blamed himself for not winning the gold medal and he suffered from depression as a result. Medvec, Madey & Giilovich (1995) found silver medalists were less satisfied with their performance than were bronze medalists, perhaps because they expected to win gold medals. Apparently each person gives himself a running commentary of his worth and a perception of low value can be destructive.

The words others say can hurt too. Charles Cooley postulated the looking glass-self theory. (Cooley, C., 1902) "He said, "You are who you think that other people think that you are". In other words he said each person defines himself with the labels others put on him. If other people tend a man that he's intelligent, honest and responsible he'll incorporate those labels in his self-image and live up to them. If others tell him he's worthless and stupid he'll believe that he's worthless and stupid. As a result of incorporating negative labels self-esteem can plummet and depression can result. Negative labeling can happen to anyone but it might be especially likely to happen to children with Asperger's Syndrome. They could be labeled by parents, teachers and classmates. *Their eccentric behavior might seem strange to others drawing negative comments*. Children with Asperger's Syndrome grow up with social rejection and they often feel unworthy. They have what used to be called an inferiority complex because others bombard them with negative messages about themselves.

Each person has a reference group, those he compares himself too. Perhaps it would be better for a child with Asperger's Syndrome to compare himself to another child with the same problem. *Perhaps students with Asperger's Syndrome should get to know each other*. Comparing one's self to super achievers is never a good idea. A child with Asperger's disorder might have low self-esteem if he compares himself to the more popular students in his class.

Negative messages can be overcome with positive ones. A child with low self-esteem can be helped if given positive messages about him-self. Parents can be very instrumental in helping them to feel better about themselves. *Praising a child for a past success can help offset negative messages from others about a present failure*. Occasions of failure can be more difficult for students already struggling to like themselves.

LOSS OF RELATIONSHIP OR LACK OF REWARD CAN CAUSE DEPRESSION

It has been hypothesized that loss of a relationship can cause depression. (Mathes, Adams & Davies, 1985) *People seem to need relationships and appear to be unhappy without them.* That explains why people seek new relationships so soon after bad relationships end. It also explains why unemployment, divorce and death can cause depression. Work isn't just a way to get money it's also a set of relationships with coworkers, supervisors and customers. When one loses a job he loses those relationships. Not going to work anymore means he doesn't see those people again. He loses part of his identity, income and relationships, making unemployment very stressful. Think of a man who works at a factory for twenty years. He sees his friends each work day and enjoys talking with them. One day the factory closes so his job ends. Social isolation begins. He finds himself home all day watching television and missing the social interaction at work that he used to have. Divorce is even more difficult because the marital relationship is so important in so many ways, especially for women. Imagine a woman who is a homemaker and has children. Her husband divorces her because he wants someone younger. Suddenly she feels loss of her identity. Not knowing who she is she has to rethink her whole life while struggling to find herself. Children also lose most of a relationship. Divorce usually means the children stay with the mother so they lose all or at least part of the relationship they had with the father. That leaves the children with a whole in their lives. Death is of course the ultimate end of a relationship. Loss of a parent not only ends a relationship but leaves things undone and words unsaid. Even the loss of a romantic relationship or a friendship can cause emotional pain. What might help is beginning a new relationship.

Loss of a relationship is a kind of rejection, especially the loss of a romantic partner. When one loses that kind of a relationship he naturally thinks about why it happened. He wonders why the other found him not good enough. That causes a loss of self-esteem. *Fear of loss of a romantic relationship explains why some people freak out when a relationship breaks up and they refuse to accept it.* That's why restraining orders are common.

People need to be rewarded from time to time but too many rewards hurt people. They naturally seek rewards and some people go over- board gorging themselves on whatever they like. *Money, sex, food, drink, artistic pursuits, praise and interesting company are the main rewards.* If someone goes a long time under difficult circumstances without reward he will become depressed. The solution is probably to get a reward. Rewarding yourself once in a while is a good idea. Some people become addicted to reward. They don't appreciate the small things so they feel driven to get as many of the big things that they can. Depression sets in if they can't get those things. That's what sex addiction is about. Some people rely on sex to avoid depression and they become depressed and anxious without it. Eventually they feel driven to meaningless and dangerous sex that leaves them feeling ashamed of themselves. Over doing a good thing is never a good idea. Think of the position of an alcoholic. He enjoyed drinking at first but eventually he had to drink even though it started to make him sick. Maybe depressed people become caught up in addiction because they go too far seeking reward to escape depression.

STRESS AND DEPRESSION

Stress can cause depression. It was found that stress caused depression in those mice that had overactive immune systems. (Hodes, 2012) An overactive immune system might have been a genetic marker for under production of serotonin. It might work the same in people. ***Those people with under production of serotonin could become depressed when subjected to stress.*** Think of a young soldier serving in a war. Each morning he goes on patrol fearing contact with the enemy. One day he encounters the enemy and a fire fight occurs. Bullets fly, mortar shells land all around, men are wounded and some die. After the fight the soldier continues to have problems with anxiety. He can't sleep or concentrate. He spends all of his time reliving what happened. Stress causes anxiety which takes its toll. Soon the soldier becomes depressed. It becomes harder and harder for him to report for duty each day and when he does he fails to perform well, seemingly not caring what happens to him or the other men around him. After two weeks he's so depressed that he can't do anything so he has to be hospitalized. Eventually he recovered but he can't be returned to combat.

Stress can cause depression for a family. Imagine a middle aged man losing his job because the factory where he works moves to China. Suddenly he has no income other than unemployment, and that doesn't last for long. He's the first one in his family to be affected by depression. Looking for work was very depressing because he went to five employers each work day and all of them told him that they weren't accepting applications. He arrived home feeling a little worse each day. Eventually he gave up looking for work, staying home and drinking instead. His wife was the next to feel it. Money ran short and debts piled up. Soon there wasn't enough money to buy adequate food and bill collectors called every day. One day she finally gave up. After that she spent all of her time watching television and wishing she were someone else. The children were the last to feel it. Arriving home from school each day they found their parents depressed and little food to eat. Finally they became depressed and starting failing in school.

Stress can cause depression for a large part of society. Think of people living in Germany during World War Two. Each day planes pounded their country with bombs night and day. There were dead bodies and fires in lots of places. No one could sleep well because they were all afraid of bombs. Food, water, fuel and medical supplies became increasingly scarce. All the people could do was live in fear. The sound of planes made it worse. They heard planes every day and every night but never knew where bombs would land. Bomb shelters were the only places they felt somewhat safe. Even they weren't completely safe because some were destroyed by bombs. Depression set in, not among everyone but only among those who under produced serotonin. Soon they weren't able to work or even to take care of themselves. Eventually they resembled the movie image of the walking dead, able to walk but not to do much more. Their inability to work helped seal the fate of their country. The point is it could happen to any country. It happened to Germany but it could happen to America. Americans could become depressed from national trauma. It happened to small number after the nine eleven attack but it could happen to a lot more if the economy were to collapse.

There is evidence that brain structure is involved in depression. *It has been discovered that a genetic difference led to larger synaptic gaps in the brains of those with depression*. (Fox News, 2012) A larger synaptic gap would undoubtedly reduce neural impulses and that might lead to depression. The brain communicates with itself by releasing chemicals called neurotransmitters into synapses, spaces between neurons. When a neuron takes up a neurotransmitter it might fire an electro-chemical charge releasing a neurotransmitter into the next synapse in a chain. If less neurotransmitter makes it across a synapse to be picked up by neighboring neurons fewer neurons will fire. Lack of neural activity might result in depression. A difference in brain structure implicates a genetic cause of depression and points to the need for a medication solution. It also provides an explanation for relapse because if depression goes away the abnormal brain structure remains and it might start the cycle of depression again.

The brains of depressed people responded less to pleasure than did the brains of normal people. (Heller, Johnstone, Shackman, Light, Peterson, Kolden, kalin, & Daviodson, 2009) *The reward center of the brain seemed to have become less active so those who were depressed experienced less pleasure*. That explained why depressed people appeared to like the pleasant little things of life. The question that was left unanswered was if depression reduced activity in the pleasure center of the brain or if a reduction in pleasure center activity led to depression. Reduced activity in the pleasure center of the brain makes it difficult to overcome depression.

Brain synchronicity is clearly involved in depression. A researcher found another interesting difference in the brains of those with depression. *They had greater synchronicity in some parts of the brain, that is different parts of the brain seemed to fire in the same way*. (Leuchter, 2012) Over synchronicity is a problem because it means the brain has difficult multi-tasking. In a normal person different parts of the brain smoothly perform different functions at the same time. Over synchronicity indicates the different parts of the brain are not operating as independently as normal. That lack of independence might mean some brain functions are not properly occurring. Apparently synchronicity is complex. It was found that the brains of those depressed were less synchronized in the hate circuit. (Tao, Guo, Ge, Kendrick, Xue, Liu, & Feng, J., 2011) The hate circuit is three parts of the brain that light up in studies of the brain function involved with the emotion of hate. *Depressed people are somewhat anti-social and have a difference in function involving the hate circuit.*

Low self-esteem led to prejudice (Psych-Central, 2012) and prejudice and depression occur together often. (Cox, Devine, & Hollon, 2012). *Maybe a loss of self-esteem increases Depression and an increase in depression causes an increase in prejudice.* People with depression have low activity in the pre-frontal cortex. (George, Ketter, & Post, 1994) If depression is the cause of prejudice perhaps horrors like the holocaust and slavery can be averted by treating depression. National depression could predict gross human rights abuses and help explain some of the things that have happened in the past. It might also point to a way to prevent genocide and slavery. It's understandable that depression can make people more difficult to get along with.

Beck, A.T. (1967). *Depression: clinical, experimental and theoretical aspects*. New York: Harper and Row.

Coloey, C. H. (1902). *Human Nature and the Social Order*. New York: Scribers.

Cox, W.T.L., Devine, PG. and Hollon, S.D. (2012). Stereotypes, Depression and Prejudice: The Integrated Perspective. *Perspective on Psychological Science*, September, e-published. DOI: 1177/1745691612455204.

Heller, A.S., Johnstone, T., Shackman, A. J., Light, S. N., Peterson, S. J., Kolden, G. G., kalin, N. H. and Davidson, R.J., (2009). Reduced capacity to sustain emotion in major depression reflects diminished maintenance of fronto-striatal brain activation. *Proceedings of the National Academy of Sciences* 106952: 2245-22450. DOI: 10.1073/pnqs.0910651106.

Fox News. (2012). Retrieved From http://www.foxnew/health/2012/08/.../how-depression-hrinks-brain.

Hodes, G. (2012). Could You be Allergic to Stress : A Possible Explanation for Depression. Mentioned in http://www.psychcentral.com/news/2012/10/16/could-you-be-allergic-to-stress.

Leuchter, A. F., Cook, I. A., Hunter, A. M., Cai. C. and Horvath, S. (2012). Resting State Quantitative Elecroencephalography Reveals Increased Neurophysiologic Connectivity in Depression. *PlOS One*, 7(2): e32508. DOI: 10.1037/journal.pone.0032508.

Mathes, E. W., Adams, H.E. and Davies, R. M. (1985). Jealousy: Loss of Relationship Rewards, Loss of Self-Esteem, Anxiety and Anger. *Journal of Personality and Social Psychology*, 48(6): 1552-1561. DOI: 10.1037/0022-3514.48.6.1552.

Medvec, V. H., Madey, S. F. and Gilovih, T. (1995). When less is more: Counterfactual thinking and satisfaction among Olympic medalists. *Journal of Personality and Social Psychology*, 69(4): 603-610. DOI: 10.11037/0022-3514.69.4.603.

Psych-Central. (2012). Retrieved From http://www.psych-central.com.news.2012/02/24/prejudice-may-stem-from-low-self-esteem23839.

Seligman, M.E.P. and Maier, S. F. (1967). Failure to Escape traumatic Shock. Journal of Experimental Psychology, 74(1): 1-9. DOI: 10.1037/h002-4514.

Tao, H., Guo, S., Ge, T., Kendrick, K. M., Xue, Z., Liu, Z. and Feng, J. (2011). Depression uncouples brain hate circuit. *Molecular Psychiatry*, e-published October, 4. DOI: 10.1038/mp.2011.127.

BIPOLAR DISORDER

Bipolar Disorder (B.P.D.) is a serious mental illness that affects increasing numbers of people. There are five types of B.P.D. (DSM-IV-TR (2000) 4th ed. text rev.) B.P.D. 1 includes severe swings from mania to depression. Mania can include delusions of grandeur and seemingly endless energy combines with risky behavior. B.P.D. 2 includes milder episodes of mania but severe depression. Cyclothymic Disorder is episodes of severe mania and mild depression. Mixed Bipolar has episodes of combined mania and depression. Rapid Cycling is four or more episodes in one year. People with B.P.D. are severely affected and require professional treatment. The incidence of B.P.D. has increased greatly. (Blanco, Jiang, Schmidt, & Olfson, 2005) Consider five examples of B.P.D. Bob has B.PD. 1. He goes through two episodes a year. Each time he starts with mania, feeling optimistic with delusions that he can accomplish anything. He sleeps much less and makes ambitious plans. Depression follows. He sleeps a lot and has no interest in anything. Janet has B.P.D. 2. She goes through periods of mild mania followed by severe depression. When depressed she's unable to work and thinks about killing herself. Devlin has Cyclothymic Disorder. He experiences severe mania, thinking he can do anything. Hyper-sexuality accompanies severe mania and he has sex up to three times a day while manic. Mania is followed by depression requiring hospitalization. Marta has Mixed B.P.D. During an episode she feels both manic and depressed at the same time, leaving her unable to function normally.

The cause of B.P.D. is unknown, but genetics, marijuana and stress play a role. Research has shown if one identical twin has B.P.D. the odds are between 40% and 70% that the other will develop it. (Craddok, & Jones, 1999) First degree relatives of those with B.P.D. are more likely to develop major depression. (Coryell, & Endicott, 1984) Marijuana smoking is much more common among those with B.P.D.. (Feinman, & Dunner, 1996) Stress seems to make B.P.D. more severe.

Those with B.P.D. have brain abnormalities. They experience shrinkage in grey matter in the prefrontal and temporal regions. (William, Moorehead, McKirdy, Sussmnn, Hall, Lawrie, Johnstone & McIntosh, 2007) They also have a loss of volume in the limbic system. (Yl, Sun, Hsiehm , 2008) Patients with B.P.D. have been shown to have abnormalities in serotonin and norepinephrine (National Center for Biological Information, 2005). The prefrontal region is involved in decision making and moderating social behavior. Lots of grey matter could lead to poor decision making and a failure to adjust social behavior, both typical of B.P.D. The temporal region is involved in processing auditory information, personality, behavior, speech, memory and visual memory. Damage to the temporal region could cause behavior problems and auditory hallucinations. The limbic system is involved in emotion. Damage to the limbic system could explain mood swings typical of B.P.D. An excess of serotonin, epinephrine and norepinephrine might overload the brain. In some ways the brain of someone with B.P.D. is similar to the brain of someone with schizophrenia. (McDonald, Bullmore, Sham, Xavier, Harvey, Braman, & Murray, 2004) Brain abnormalities point to the possibility of early diagnosis.

B.PD. can be treated with medication and counseling. Lithium helps stabilize mood, avoiding extremes. (O'Conell, Mayo, Flatow, Cuthbertson, & O'Brien, 1991) Antipsychotics can be used to treat B.P.D. (Web MD. 2011) and anticonvulsants can help treat those people who have mixed episodes. Medscape, 2003) Benzodiazepines are useful to treat anxiety, which can typically accompanies B.P.D.. (Panic Disorder, 2009) Cognitive therapy has been shown to reduce relapse (National Center for Biological Information, 2005)

American Psychiatric Association, (2000). *Diagnostic and statistical manual of mental disorders*. (4th ed., text rev.) Washington, DC: author. DOI: 10.1176/appibooks.9780890423349.

Blanco, C., Jiang, H., Schmidt, A.B. and Olfson, M, (2007). National Trends in the Outpatient Diagnosis and Treatment of Bipolar Disorder in Youth. *Archives of General Psychiatry*, 64(9): 1032-1039. DOI: 10.1001/archpshych.64.9.1032.

Bipolar. (2012). Retrieved From http://www.bipolar.about.com/od/benzodiazepines.

Craddok, N. and Jones, I. (1999). Genetics of Bipolar Disorder. *Journal of Medical Genetics*, 36: 585-594.

Feinman, J.A. and Dunner, D.L. (1996). The effect of alcohol and substance abuse on the course of bipolar affective disorder. *Journal of Affective Disorders*, 37(1): 43-49. DOI: 10.1016/0165-0327(95)00080-1.

O'Conell, R.A., Mayo, J.A., Flatow, L., Cuthbertson, B. and O'Brien. B.E. (1991). Outcome of bipolar disorder on long-term treatment with lithium. *British Journal of Psychiatry*, 159: 123-129. DOI: 10.1016/0165-0327(9)90103-Y.

Medscape. (2003) Retrieved From http://www.medscape.org/viewarticles/458701).

National Center for Biological Information. (2005). Retrieved From http://www.ncbi,nim.gov/pubmed/15677598.

National Center for Biological Information. (2005). Retrieved From http://www.ncbi.nom.gov/pubmed/18402623.

Panic Disorder. (2009). Retrieved From http://www.panicdisorder.com/od/treatments/a/t/benzos.

Web MD. (2011). Retrieved From http://www.webmd.com/bipolar-disorder/antipsychotic-medication.

William, T., Moorehead, J., McKirdy, J., Sussmann, J.E.D., Hall, J., Lawrie, S.M. and Johnstone, C.E. and McIntosh, A.M., (2007). Progressive Grey Matter Loss in Patients with Bipolar Disorder. *Biological Psychiatry*, 62(8): 894-400. DOI: 10.1016/j.biopsych.2007.03.005.

YI, L., Sun, Y.N., Hsieh, J.C. and Su, T.P., (2008). Cortical complexity analysis of patients with bipolar disorder using three-dimensional gyrification index. *Journal of Psychiatry*, 160(9): 1606-1632.

ATTENTION DEFICIT HYPERACTIVITY DISORDER

A.D.D.H.D. CAN MAKE CHILDHOOD MORE DIFFICULT

Some children are fidgety and have trouble paying attention. That problem continues into adulthood. ***Attention deficit hyperactivity disorder can be a serious problem for a child struggling to succeed in school or an adult trying to succeed at work.*** Some people have either attention deficit disorder or hyperactivity but they often go together and unfortunately those people with Asperger's Syndrome might have a high rate of both. (Mazzone, Ruta, & Reale, 2012) Imagine yourself as an eight year old with both problems. You sit in a small desk in a crowded room and constantly feel uncomfortable. Filled with energy you want to get up and do something, but you know that you can't because if you do your teacher will be angry with you and your classmates will think you're strange. Often times your attention wonders during class. You think about other things, perhaps imagining you're someone else in an exciting adventure or may just zone out not really thinking of anything. Suddenly you awaken to realize you missed the whole lesson. You do badly on the next test as a result. As hard as you try you just can't pay attention for more than five minutes. Now think of yourself as an adult. You can work harder than your co-workers because they get tired and you don't, so you can easily out produce them. That works as long as you don't have a detailed job that requires you to sit at a desk. You might also multi-task well because you can easily shift your attention back and forth between tasks as long as they don't require too much detail work.

Parents and teachers have tried to understand attention deficit hyperactivity disorder through the years. Some thought it was boredom or lack of motivation. Diet was discussed. Others thought all that was needed was some strenuous exercise to burn excess energy. Still it remained a bit of a mystery. Some research indicates under stimulation might be the cause. (Prediger et al, 2005) Rats with attention deficit hyperactivity disorder experienced significantly improved performance when given caffeine. Anecdotal evidence suggests the same often happens in people. It's possible that instead of being overstimulated those with the disorder are under-stimulated, so perhaps it's an extreme form of boredom. Segal, M., 2008 discovered evidence that the disorder might be the result of overstimulation. His theory was overactive ion channels in the muscles bombarded the brain with stimuli when potassium levels in the blood were low. ***Parents' were left confused wondering if attention deficit hyperactivity disorder was the result of under stimulation or overstimulation and if it could be treated with caffeine or potassium.***

When someone has Asperger's Syndrome the last thing he needs is another problem. Asperger's Syndrome is difficult enough. Trying to fit in with peers is difficult for an autistic and even more so if he can't pay attention. It's also a problem for teachers. ***Teaching a student with Asperger's Syndrome is tough but if he also has attention deficit hyperactivity disorder it's much tougher.*** Each disorder requires classroom time and that's something teachers are always short of so students with special needs get short changed in favor of other students. Mixing regular and special needs students can be both good and bad.

The best understanding of the brain with attention deficit disorder is that it contains a genetic fault. A defective gene or genes seems to be responsible for abnormal physical development of the brain in those with the disorder. That abnormal development causes symptoms which have been labeled as the disorder. ***Parents can be held accountable for how they help children with the disorder but not for causing attention deficit hyperactivity disorder.*** It's not possible to change brain structure but medication may help. Having realistic expectations is also important. Children with e disorder need to be raised differently.

The brains of those with the disorder are different. Filipek, Semrod-Clikerman, Steingard, Renshaw, Kennedy & Beiderman, J., (1997) found those with attention deficit disorder had structural brain differences including smaller volume in the left caudate region and the right anterior-superior region. The caudate nucleus is involved in learning to read a second language. (Tan, Chen, Yip, Chan, Yang, Gao, & Siok, 2010). The right anterior-superior region is involved in comprehending spoken language. (Crinion, & Price, 2005) Those deficits point to extreme difficulty among those afflicted in learning foreign languages. Anatomical brain differences indicate a possible genetic cause of the disorder. That was reinforced by a finding that those with attention deficit disorder had delayed development of the cortical surface of the brain. (Shaw, 2012). Lack of dopanergic activity in the brain could go a long ways toward explaining attention deficit disorder and the high risk behavior that often accompanies it. Researchers found the brains of those with the disorder had lower dopamine activity in the reward center of the brain. (Volkow, Wang, Kollins, Wigal, Newcorn, Telang, Ma, Pradhan, Wong, & Swanson, 2009) Lack of dopamine activity results in lack of reward. Lack of reward logically leads to inattention, explaining the principle symptom of the disorder. ***It explains something else at least as important. Those with attention deficit disorder often fall victim to high risk behavior possibly including ambling, drug use and sexual promiscuity.*** Hallowell, & Ratey, (1994) showed those with attention deficit disorder had less blood flow and less glucose utilization in the prefrontal cortex. The prefrontal cortex is involved in decision making and that might explain why people with the disorder often have trouble making good decisions. Children with attention deficit disorder frequently misbehave, seeing to have greater difficulty than other children in learning how to act. That could contribute to risk taking behavior in adulthood.

Patience and consistency are especially important for parents of children with the disorder. The children have greater difficulty learning because of a brain problem so they will need extra help. Most frustratingly they will need extra help learning to think of consequences and making good decisions. That will be very important in the future because without it they will likely develop serious behavior problems that could ruin their lives and lead them into trouble with the law. ***Teachers need to be aware that children with attention deficit hyperactivity disorder aren't likely willfully defiant, but much more likely have difficulty learning to associate behavior with consequences.***

Crinion, J. and Price, C.J., (2005). Right anterior superior temporal activation predicts auditory sentence comprehension following aphasic stroke. *Brain*, 128(12): 2858-2871. DOI: 10.1093/brain/awh659.

Fillipek, P.A., Semrud-Clikeman, M., Steingard, R.J., Renshaw, P.F., Kennedy, D.N. and Biederman, J., (1997). Volumetric MRI analysis comparing subjects having attention-deficit hyperactivity disorder with normal controls. *Neurology*, 48: 589-601. DOI: 10.1212/WNL.48.3.589.

Mazzone, L., Ruta, L. and Reale, L., (2012). Psychiatric comorbidities in asperger syndrome and high functioning autism: diagnostic challenges. *Annals of general Psychiatry*, 11(16): e-published. DOI: 10.1186/1744-859X-11-16.

Prediger, R.D.S., Pamplona, F.A., Fernandes, D. and Takahashi, R.N., (2005). Caffeine improves spatial learning deficits in an animal model of attention deficit hyperactivity disorder (ADHD) – the spontaneously hyperactive rat (SHR). *The International Journal of Nueropsychopharmacology*, 8(4); 583-594. DOI: 10.11017/S1461145705005341.

Ratey, J.J. and Hallowell, L.M., (1995). Relationships Dilemmas for Adults with ADD: *The Biology of Intimacy*. Brunner/Mazel, New York: New York.

Tan, L.H., Chen, L., Yip, V., Chan, A.H.D., Jang, J., Gao, J. and Siok, W.T., (2011). Activity levels in the left hemisphere caudate-fusiform circuit predict how well a second language will be learned. *Proceedings of the National Academy of Sciences*, 108(6): 2540-2544. DOI: 10.1073/pnas.09090623108.

Volkow, N. D., Wang, G., Kollins, S. H., Wigal, T. L., Newcorn, J. H., Telang, F., Ma, Y., Pradhan, K., Wong, C. and Swanson, J. M., (2009). Evaluating Dopamine Reward Pathway in ADHD Clinical Implications. *Journal of the American Medical Association*, 302(10): 1084-1091. DOI: 10.1001/jama.2009.1308.

DYSPRAXIA

Dyspraxia is also known as clumsy child syndrome. It's a brain dysfunction that causes uncoordinated movement. *Dyspraxia is an immaturity of the brain that interferes with processing of information about physical movement.* Some people with the disorder outgrow out. Coordination requires both hemispheres of the brain to work together. The right hemisphere controls the left side of the body and the left hemisphere controls the left side of the body. Dyspraxia might result from damage to the left hemisphere of the brain. (Kimura, 1977) Clumsiness is of course the symptom of the disorder. Dyspraxia appears to be caused by slow development of motor neurons in the brain which control movement. It might be caused by genetics, premature birth, alcohol or tobacco. (National Health Service, 2012)

Think of Jim, a seven year old with dyspraxia. He wants to play sports with his friends but every time he tries he does poorly because he's clumsy. *That points to what is probably the biggest problem with dyspraxia, social isolation.* He tried hard at baseball, but he has trouble catching, throwing and batting. Being clumsy he sometimes falls, especially on stairs. Jim will have to overcome clumsiness if he is to play sports latter.

Therapy can help. An occupation therapist could aid a patient in developing coordination to perform everyday tasks. (Schaaf & Miller, 2005) Some patients with the disorder have trouble with speech because of coordination problems so a speech therapist might be able to help. (Rosenbeck, Lemme, Ahern, & Harris, 1973) Perceptual motor training can also help. (Davidson, Brian, 2000) Medication plays no role in treating dyspraxia.

Kimura, D., (1977). ACQUISITION OF A MOTOR SKILL AFTER LEFT HEMISPHERE DAMAGE. *Brain*, 100: 527-542.

National Helath Service. (2012). Retrieved From http://www.nhs.uk/Conditions/Dyspraxia-(childhood)/Pages/Causes.aspx.

Rosenbeck, J.C., Lemme, M.L., Ahern, M.B. and Harris, E.H., 1973). A treatment for apraxia of speech in adults. *Journal of Speech and Hearing Disorders*, 38: 462-472.

Schaaf, R.C. and Miller, L.J., (2005). Occupational therapy using a sensory integrative approach for children with developmental disabilities. *Mental Retardation and Developmental Disabilities research Review*, 11(2): 143-148. DOI: 10.1002/mrdd.20067.

TOURETTE'S SYNDROME

Tourette's Syndrome (T.S.) is a brain dysfunction that causes involuntary movements and vocalizations. (DSM-IV-TR (2000) 4th ed. text rev.) Motor tics can include eye blinking, facial grimacing, head jerking and shoulder jerking. Vocalizations could include repetitive throat clearing, sniffing or grunting. Some people with T.S. speak inappropriate words, for example swear language or threats. T.S. can include attacks of rage. Contrary to commons sense people with T.S. have greater cognitive control of motor movements. A genetic fault might cause T.S. because it is associated with brain abnormality. (Pourfar, Feigin, Tang, Carbon-Correll, Bussa, Budman, Dhawan, & Eidelberg, 2011). Histamine might play a role in T.S. (Scientific American, 2011).

Consider Andrew, a young man with T.S. He exhibits eye blinking and grunting. Those symptoms make it very difficult for him to meet new people of work. Whenever he meets people all they seem to notice is his rapid eye blinking and grunting, which they don't understand. ***As a result they are afraid of him.*** He has the same problem at every job interview so no one will hire him. Given a chance he would be a good friend and a good employee. Life seems very unfair.

T.S. can be treated with medication and therapy. Antipsychotic medication that partially blocks the effect of dopamine can reduce symptoms of T.S. (Nervous System, 2009) but have side effects. An injection of botulism toxin can reduce vocal tics. (Salloway, Stewart, Israeli, Morales, Rasmussen, Blitzer & Brain, 1996) Central adrenergic inhibitors can help to control rage. (Mayo Clinic, 2012) Behavior therapy can reduce vocal and physical tics. (Reese, Timpano, Siev, Rowley & Wilhelm, 2010).

American Psychiatric Association, (2000). *Diagnostic and statistical manual of mental disorders.* (4th ed., text rev.) Washington, DC: author. DOI: 10.1176/appibooks.9780890423349.

Pourfar, M., Feigin, A., TANG, C.C., Carbon-Correll, M., Bussa, M., Budman, C., Dhawan, C. and Eidelberg, C., (2011). Abnormal metabolic brain networks in Tourette syndrome. *Neurology*, 76(11): 944-52.

Mayo Clinic. (2012). Retrieved From http://www.mayoclinic.com'health/tourettes-syndrome/D500541/DSECTION=treatments-and-drugs.

Nervous System, (2009). Retrieved From http://www.nervous-system.emedtv.com/tourettes-syndrome-treatment.

Reese, H.E., Timpano, K.R., Siev, J., Rowley, T. and Wilhelm, S., (2010). Behavior Therapy for Tourette's Syndrome and Chronic tic Disorder: A Web Based Video Illustration of Treatment Components. *Cognitive and Behavioral Practice*, 17(1): 16-24.

Salloway, S., Stewart, C.F., Israeli, L., Morales, X., Rasmussen, S., Blitzer, A., and Brain, M.F., (1996). Botuliminm toxin for refractory vocal tics. *Movement Disorders*, Nov, 4, DOI;10.1002/mds.8701.10627.

Scientific American. (2011). Retrieved From http://www.scienticamerican.com/articles.cfn?id=treating-tourettes.

ALCOHOLISM

Alcoholism occurs frequently in families with Autistic Spectrum Disorders. (Miles, Takahashi, Haber & Hadden, 2003) There might be three reasons for that. There could be a common genetic link, anxiety associated with A.S. might lead to alcoholism and depression which is LAO associated with A.S. could do the same. *What is certain is people with A.S. are at high risk for alcohol addiction so they need to be careful when drinking.* The brain of someone predisposed to develop alcoholism is different making a genetic link possible. Researchers have found 40% to 60% of the risk of developing alcoholism is genetic. (Heath, Madden, Bucholz, Dinwidde, Slutske, Bierut, Rohrbaugh, Statham, Dunne, Whitfield,... Martin, 1999) Those with a family history of alcoholism showed reduced P300 amplitude when making decisions about task related stimuli. (O'Connor, Hesselbrok, Tasman & DePalma, 1987). That indicated a difference in the way their brains functioned. Alleles can predict reaction to alcohol, possibly putting some people at risk. (Xinazhang, Oroszi, Chun, Smith, Goldman & Schucikt, 2006) An allele is a variation of a gene, for example one variation of the same gene causes blue eyes and another causes green eyes. Subjects who react less to alcohol; indicating greater tolerance are at greater risk. People with a family history of alcoholism show increased sensitivity to ethanol in the pituitary b-endorphin system. (Gianoulakis, Beliveau, Angelogianni, Meaney, Thavundayil & Tawar, 1989). Endorphins are natural opiate like chemicals that reduce pain and produce euphoria. Someone predisposed to alcoholism apparently produces more endorphins in response to alcohol than other people do. The increased production of endorphins makes drinking more pleasurable. Researchers found it was common for people with anxiety disorders to use alcohol as self-medication. (Kushner, Abrams & Borchardt, 2000) Anxiety could drive alcohol consumption propelling people toward alcoholism. Social isolation often accompanies A.S. and it could lead to excessive alcohol consumption.

Take Dan for example. He is in his late twenties and has A.S. as well as anxiety and depression. *Anxiety makes it hard for him to work or do the normal things of life.* It's like a curse that plagues him all of the time. Being afraid of antianxiety medication because his mother had problems with it he relies on alcohol. He's stressed out by the time he gets home from work every day so all he can think of doing is drinking two doubles brandies. It's worse on the weekends because work helps limit his drinking on weekdays. On a typical weekend he has seven or eight drinks each day. Depression is part of the issue. Dan sees little reason not to drink because his depression causes him to care little about life and himself. It makes planning for the future impossible. If the present trend continues Dan will become alcoholic.

Alcoholism can be treated with therapy, medication and participation in self-help group activities but it is best not to become alcoholic. Naltrexone could be combined with cognitive behavioral therapy for the treatment for alcoholism. Participation in Alcoholic Anonymous might help. Alcoholics Anonymous provides alcoholics with an opportunity to share their experiences and encourage each other in sobriety.

Gianoulakis, C., Beliveau, D., Angelogianni, P., meaney, M., Thavundayil, J. and Tawar, D.M., (1989). Different pituitary B-endorphin and adrenal cortisol response to ethanol individuals with high and low risk for future development of alcoholism. *Life Sciences*, 45(12): 1097-1109.
DOI: 10.1016/0024-32059(89)90167-7.

Heath, A.C., Madden, P.A.F., Bucholz, C.C., Dinwidde, S.H., Slutske, W.S., Bierut, L.J., Rohrbaugh, J.W., Statham, D.J., Dunne, M.P., Whitfield, J.B. and Martin, N.G., (1999). Genetic sensitivity in alcohol and the inheritance of alcohol risk. *Psychological medicine*, 29(5): 1069-1081.

Kushner, M.G., Abrams, K. and Borchardt, C., (2000). The relationship between anxiety disorders and alcohol use disorders: A review of major perspectives and findings. *Clinical Psychology Review*, 20(2): `49-171.

Miles, J. H., Takahashi,N., Haber, A. and Hadden, L., (2003). Autism Families with a High Incidence of Alcoholism. *Journal of Autism and Developmental Disorders*, 33(4): 403-415,
DOI: 10.1023/A:1025010828304.

O'Connor, S., Hesselbrok, V., Tasman, A., and DePalma, N., (1987). P3 amplitudes in two distinct tasks are decreased in young men with a history of paternal alcoholism. *Alcohol*, 4(4): 323-330.

Xinazhang, H., Oroszi, G., Chun J., Smith, T.., Goldman, D. and Schucikt, M.A., (2006). An Expanded Evaluation of the Relationship of Four Alleles to the Level of Response to Alcohol and Alcoholism Risk. Alcoholism: *Clinical and Experimental Research*, 29(1): 8-16,
DOI: 10.1097/01.ALC.0000150008.68473.62.

HIGH FUNCTIONING AUTISM

High Functioning Autism (H.F.A.) is similar to A.S. and in fact the two disorders are often confused. H.F.A. is high functioning in a person who exhibits symptoms of autism. High functioning could mean an I.Q. of at least 80. (DSM-IV-TR (2000) text-rev.) Those with A.S. might be more intelligent. A key difference is people with A.S. didn't have delayed language development, more trouble with visual-spatial perception and visual-motor coordination (DSM-IV-TR (2000) text rev.). *The two disorders are clearly closely related, but perhaps the most important difference is those with A.S. have a much better prognosis.*

It's easier to see the difference between H.F.A. and A.S. when they are compared side by side. Imagine Albert, a fifteen year old with H.F.A. He shows clear signs of autism and has average intelligence. His studies are going alright but he is only a "C" student. His greatest problem is social isolation because he doesn't get along well with others and seems to prefer being alone. It's likely he will graduate from high school but probably end up in an unskilled job. Think of Jamie, a fifteen year old with A.S. Like Albert he has trouble making friends but unlike Albert he is very intelligent. As an honor student he's looking forward to studying engineering after finishing high school. Unlike Albert Jamie loved to talk to adults when he was small and he was also somewhat clumsy.

American Psychiatric Association, (2000). *Diagnostic and statistical manual of mental disorders.* (4th ed., text rev.) Washington, DC: author. DOI: 10.1176/appibooks.9780890423349.

NONVERBAL LEARNING DISABILITY

A BRAIN DISORDER WITH SEVERAL SYMPTOMS

Nonverbal learning disability (N.L.D.) is a condition that impairs learning, is typically accompanied by emotional problems, is similar to Asperger's Syndrome and is caused by a brain dysfunction. Those with the disability have difficulty seeing the big picture, trouble using nonverbal communication, difficulty making friends, trouble writing, difficulty with math, trouble reading and are logically inflexible. (Smart Kids, 2013). Reading comprehension is also poor. (Slide Share, 2010) Those with N.L.D. are more likely than normal to experience anxiety and depression. (NLD Ontario, 2007) *Symptoms are eerily similar to A.S., so the two conditions are often confused.* Both are very verbal. (NLD Ontario, 2004) There is considerable overlap between the two. Right hemisphere dysfunction is involved in both conditions. (NLD Ontario, 2004) Rourke (1995) hypothesized that N.L.D. was caused by diffuse damage to white matter throughout the brain. White matter could be thought of as the wiring that makes the brain work. It connects grey matter so one part of the brain can communicate with another. (Wise Geek, 2003) N.L.D. might be the result of lack on integrated thought because of a wiring issue. It could be thought of as brain confusion.

The two conditions are different. Semrud-Clikeman and Fine (2011) found evidence that those with NLD were more likely to have cysts in the occipital/cerreblar and the parietal regions of the brain. Those regions are involved with visual-spatial perception. People with NLD typically have difficulty with visual-spatial perception and those with A.S. usually don't. A key difference is those with N.L.D. have a normal range of emotions and those with A.S. don't. Also those with A.S. have more restricted interests. (NLD Ontario, 2004) A child with A.S. lacks imaginative play but a child with N.L.D. doesn't. Children with A.S. have difficulty playing with toys. A child with N.L.D. can use language better to communicate ideas and thoughts. (Asperger Advice, 2007) N.L.D. might be a milder form of A.S., but perhaps more likely it's a different problem that has similar symptoms.

Consider Len. He's an even year old with N.L.D. *His parents began to suspect he had a problem earlier this year when he was afflicted with terrible anxiety.* It first showed up as panic attacks which started to occur in school. After three visits with a school counselor he was evaluated by a psychologist who diagnosed him with N.L.D. The diagnosis seemed to make sense. He had a great vocabulary, seemed intelligent and had always done well in school before. Now, for the first time, he was having trouble understanding what he read and completing word problems in math. Len has only one friend and often seems to miss the big picture. At first the psychologist who diagnosed him thought he had A.S. It became clear he didn't because he experienced a full range of emotions and sometimes enjoyed imaginative play. His difficulty using nonverbal communication alerted the psychologist to the possibility of A.S., but his lack of a consuming interest pointed to N.L.D. Since being diagnosed Len has started to show signs of depression. It's hard for him to get out of bed in the morning to make it to school on time and he doesn't seem to enjoy anything.

Someone with N.L.D. can be helped by therapy, but not medication must be considered individually. Auditory, speech, cognitive and social skills therapy might help. Cognitive therapy might help someone with N.L.D. to control anxiety and depression. Social skills therapy could help to make friends. Medication might reduce symptoms of A.D.D. which could also be present or might be used to reduce anxiety or depression. There is no specific medicine for N.L.D.

A teacher of a student with N.L.D. must confront incomprehension and bullying. A student might need a teacher to go over the instructions a second time or more and to question him to make sure he understands them. It might help to have a student read out loud and reread material to understanding the meaning. Students should be taught to convert a word problem into an equation. Teachers need to discourage bullying which is common with N.L.D. students. Students with N.L.D. typically face exclusion and teachers could help them find friends.

Parents of a child with N.L.D. can also help. They can teach their children to understand nonverbal communication and help them to make friends. Also they can communicate with teachers often and help their children to practice reading comprehension during summer breaks. Encouraging them to participate in extracurricular activities might be questionable. It could provide opportunities to make friends, but it could also add stress which might result in anxiety. Participation in an activity club might make more sense. Reassurance would no doubt help a child facing social exclusion.

Asperger Advice. (2007). Retrieved From http://www.asperger-advice.com/nonverbal-learning-disorder.

NLD Ontario. (2004). Retrieved From http://www.nodontario/articles/NLDvsAS.

NLD Ontario. (2007). Retrieved From http://www.nldontario.org/artcles/HlpingNLD.

Rourke, B.P. (1995). Syndrome of Nonverbal Learning Disabilities: Neuraldevelopmental Manifestations. Guilford Press. New York: New York.

Semrud-Clikeman, M. and Fine, J. (2011). Presence of Cysts on Magnetic Image Resonance Images (MRIs) in Children With Asperger Disorder and Nonverbal Learning Disabilities. Journal of Child Neurology, 26.4: 471-475. DOI: 10.1177/0883073810384264.

Slide Share. (2010). Retrieved From http://www.slideshare.net.../understanding –nonverbal-learning-disability.

Smart Kids. (2013). Retrieved From http://www.smartkidswith.org/ld...symptoms/signs-symptoms-of-nld.

Wise Geek. (2003). Retrieved From http://www.wisegeek.com/what-is-the-function-of-white-matter-in-the-brain.

SUMMING UP

A.S. is a recognized disorder causing childhood difficulties but often leading to career success. Those people with A.S. are different. They exhibit eccentric behavior, and are typically intelligent, often with special talents (DSM-IV-TR (2000). Text rev.) They have trouble with communication , often have physical problems and often have other problems (DSM-IV,TR (2000) text rev). Their biggest problem is making friends. (Life With Asperger's, 2007) Mental health professionals have known about A.S. for a long time, but it only became a recognized disorder in 1994. (DSM-IV-TR (2000) text. rev.) Those with A.S. typically have difficult childhoods. They typically struggle very hard socially, are often bullied and have trouble understanding others. Making friends is difficult because they have trouble feeling empathy. (DSM-IV-TR (2000) text rev.) They are often bullied because they are different. It's hard for them to communicate because they use literal language and don't use body language. People with A.S. often have very successful careers because many are intelligent and have special talents but also because they have unusual focus. Career possibilities include science, engineering, medicine, music, writing and foreign languages.

Anxiety and depression commonly afflict those with A.S. (Tantam, 1999) Severe anxiety beginning at puberty is typical. That makes life much more difficult for those who suffer with the disorder. It adds an extra problem that confuses those with A.S. At that age a great many don't know that they have A.S. and fewer understand it. All they know is they are different from other people and have more problems. The anxiety they experience manifests itself as various disorders. Perhaps most baffling for them is they have no idea why they experience so much anxiety. There doesn't have to be a triggering event. Anxiety can seemingly come out of nowhere. Moderate depression is yet another malady associated with A.S. Facing up to problems is more difficult with depression.

A.D.D. and Hyperactivity add to the problems of A.S. Someone with A.S. might have problems at school. Not paying attention in class could lead low grades and that might lead to conflicts with teachers. Hyperactivity could also cause problems with teachers. Imagine a child with A.S., A.D.D.H.D. In school he keeps getting out of his seat because he can't stand to sit still for long periods of time. His teacher gets angry with him because he walks around the room and does poorly on tests.

Lots of people with A.S. think of childhood as they difficult time and carry scares from what they go through. Instead of being filled with fond memories it's full of strife, anxiety and depression. They feel different, have trouble making friends and struggle to communicate. Perhaps the lack of a happy childhood hurts them throughout life. Not having made good friends in childhood perhaps they can't make good friends as adults. Without fond memories maybe it's more difficult for them to face adult problems. Difficulty dating in the teenage years could easily make marriage tougher. Not having had a successful childhood might make parenting a bigger challenge. Perhaps difficulty getting along with teachers in childhood makes it more difficult to get along with bosses in adulthood. Trouble getting along with peers in childhood might make for trouble getting along with co-workers in adulthood.

Career success can provide a respite for those with A.S., something in their lives that they can take pride in. High intelligence, special talents and intense focus on a single topic typically provides an edge. That's especially true for those with careers in science and engineering. Imagine a violinist with A.S. who spends all of his time thinking about music. He loves music and plays for a symphony. His work is respected and he's well paid. The money he makes helps him to feel better about himself. Work is the focus of his life and defines who he is. When describing himself his job is what he mentions first.

Marriage is tough for people with A.S. They are socially immature and have communication problems. Social immaturity is the result of lack of experience interacting with the opposite sex. Lots of them grow up without really understanding the opposite sex and never learning the rules of dating. That makes it very difficult for them to successfully date as adults. It also makes them feel uneasy in dating situations. Communication is a problem for lots of couples. Men communicate well with men and women communicate well with women but men and women don't seem to naturally communicate well with each other. It's a skill they have to learn. People with A.S. don't usually learn that skill because they lack experience dating. Communication skills are critically important because all couples have conflicts and without communication skills it's very difficult to resolve conflicts. Trouble understanding nonverbal communication would make that even more difficult. Small conflicts other couples could easily work through might be big conflicts for a couple with A.S. Big conflicts could quickly lead to divorce. That explains why people with A.S. have a high rate of divorce. (Health Guide Info, 2011)

Parenting is also tough. Lots of parents have difficulty understanding their children and surely that is more difficult for those with A.S. Lack of childhood success is another factor. So is lack of empathy. Children and adults communicate differently. Effective parents must understand how to communicate with children. Parents who can't understand their children and who can't make their children understand them have lots of trouble. Lack of childhood success could make it much more difficult to prepare children for the challenges they will face. It's very important for parents to feel empathy for their own children because it's much harder to provide basic care and give enough attention without it. No doubt those with A.S. can be taught to be sensitive to the needs of children.

Alcohol can make A.S. worse because it can make anything worse. A.S. often occurs with severe anxiety (Tantum, 1999) and anxiety problems increase the risk of alcoholism (CNN, 2011). Abuse of alcohol makes marriage, parenting and work more difficult. It causes conflict, reduces the ability to deal with conflict and interferes with work. Think of someone with A.S. who suffers from anxiety and drinks as a result. He is an engineer but is in danger of losing his job because he drinks during the day and that has led to absenteeism and poor job performance. When he is at home his wife yells at him because she knows he's in danger of losing his job and all he seems to do is sit in front of a T.V. and drink. His children are angry with him because he drinks and that makes him act mean to them. Alcohol might also make him neglectful.

Adults can help children with A.S. They can teach them how to communicate and get along with others. Another way to help is to encourage them to develop their talents. It's important to teach them how to deal with anxiety, depression and the other problems that are associated with A.S. *With help children with A.S. can become successful.*

The future is in question because it's scheduled to be derecognized in 2012. *After May of that year those with A.S. will be considered normal as A.S. will no longer be listed as a disorder.* That could lead to a huge decline in research into the disorder. It might also result in a huge decrease in funding for programs to help children with A.S.

American Psychiatric Association, (2000). *Diagnostic and statistical manual of mental disorders.* (4th ed., text rev.) Washington, DC: author. DOI: 10.1176/appibooks.9780890423349.

CNN. (2011). Retrieved From http://www.cnn.com/2011/HEALTH/08/01/alcohol.anxiety.../index.

Tantam, D., 1989. Psychological Disorders in Adolescents and Adults with Asperger Syndrome. *Autism*, 4(1): 47-62, DOI: 10/1177/136236300004001004.

HOW ASPIE ADULTS CAN HELP THEMSELVES

STRESS MANAGEMENT AND CAREER CHOICE ARE KEY

Some Aspies are successful and others aren't. The way they manage their problems might be what makes the difference. They face four major challenges. *Aspies must manage stress, choose the right career, choose the right partner if they decide to marry and physically develop.* Self-advocacy is also a good idea. Each challenge requires a well thought out plan.

Stress management is critical. Aspies who don't follow a stress management program are likely to become overwhelmed by anxiety. Anxiety can make life horrible, and even if it doesn't become that bad it can certainly damage career and marriage. Managing stress is like filling a glass with water one tea spoon at a time in that it requires several steps, each of which is ineffective on its own, but they are very effective if done together. It's best to think of the steps as rules. The first rule is to make time for sleep. A lack of sleep aggravates anxiety. Second is to take some time to relax and have fun. Over worked people are stressed out. Third is to exercise. Aerobic exercise is a good friend for those who suffer from anxiety. Fourth is to use a relaxation method. Systematic relaxation, meditation, self-hypnosis and biofeedback can be good choices. The fifth is to avoid a low fat diet. The last is to avoid stress. For someone with road rage, that means riding trains. Avoiding a high stress job is very important. Medication might be needed to supplement stress management. Rational emotive therapy could also be used.

A.S. limits career choices because of discrimination, the need to limit stress and difficulty with social interaction. Social interaction problems could make a career in sales tough. Military service, law enforcement, firefighting and health care might be too stressful. Aspies face discrimination due to public ignorance and that makes it difficult for them to find jobs. Those with degrees typically find work in engineering, science, math, the computer professions, teaching higher education, art or translating foreign languages. Those without degrees might find work in the trades, technical positions or office positions. Homemaking is also possible, and should be considered a semi-profession because it requires a small amount skill at many activities and because it requires a professional attitude and continuing learning to do well. A special interest or a special talent can lead to a career.

Some Aspies experience career failure, possibly working at one hundred or more jobs without succeeding at any of them. That most likely happens because they chose the wrong careers, aren't fully prepared for work or they have difficulty getting along with supervisors and coworkers. Getting along on a job is just as important as doing the job well. People with A.S. have trouble getting along with others because of communication difficulties. They might rigidly follow rules which could also cause conflict. The last big career pitfall they have is not practicing for interviews. Aspies aren't naturally good at nonverbal communication and nonverbal cues often determine who will get hired so they need to practice interviewing with someone who can give them constructive advice. Discrimination makes it imperative for Aspies to go into careers that have shortages of workers.

Dating is very difficult for Aspies. Some are never sexually active, others date and some marry but face the risk of divorce. Successful dating requires four skills, presentation management, communication, conflict resolution and the ability to follow dating rules. *Failure at any of the four can lead to dating disaster*. Impression management has a lot to do with appearance, but also with speech and topics of conversation. There will be no second dates for those who have bad first dates. Aspies might not be good at impression management so practice could help. Happy couples communicate well. Talking is not as easy as it seems. Men and women communicate differently. (Sherwood, 2012) Men are much more interested in action and status and women are more interested in relationships. A common problem for men is not understanding that when women talk about problems that doesn't mean that want men to fix them. Women have a common problem of not understanding that men don't like to communicate if there's nothing wrong with a relationship. A third common couple communication problem is fighting over a disguised issue. Fighting to determine the balance of power in a relationship is very common. Men seem to have an instinctual need to feel dominant in male female relationships. An example of fighting over power is a couple who goes out to dinner and argues about what o order. The man might say to the woman that she can have anything she wants except pizza. Pizza might be what the woman says she wants. Their argument isn't about pizza, it's about power. Win-win communication helps couples to get along better. The goal is to reach agreements that give both partners what they want. (Mind Tool, 1996) It can usually be done, but a little creativity is required. A couple needing to negotiate should stick to the issue and avoid personal attacks. Each partner should know what he wants and what he really needs. Some conflicts are important and can't be resolved. In that case the relationship should end, preferably on a friendly basis. (Dating Rules, 2012) All men have difficulty understanding women, Aspies in particular because nonverbal communication is very important in romantic relationships. It's also important to realize that people don't always mean what they say. A common dating mistake of Aspies is to become sexually involved in order to have a relationship. Some are desperate to date and see themselves as having little else to offer.

One important dating question for Aspies is when to self-disclose. The partner is a serious relationship defiantly has a right to know. *It would be a good idea to disclose on the fourth date.* Disclosure should include providing basic information about A.S. Providing written material would be helpful, but not providing an expensive book as it might not be returned.

Couples often have problems talking about the big issues. A list of the most important questions follows. *One question should be discussed each week, starting with the fifth date.* It would be best for each partner to write an answer for each question because the answers will be more honest that way. One must know what he wants and can offer. Sample questions follow.

Most Aspies lack dating experience so they have difficulty thinking of things to do on dates. A variety of activities is a good idea as doing the same thing over and over becomes tiresome. Newspapers sometimes list ideas. A list of ideas follows.

COURTSHIP QUESTIONS

1. How will you make decisions? Will one person be the leader? Will each person be in charge of different things? Will decisions be made together? What will happen if you disagree?
2. Will the wife have a career outside the home? Will it be full-time or part-time? Will it include overtime and travel? Will the wife work when children are small? Will she work before there are children?
3. Who will be responsible for doing what homemaking work?
4. How clean do you want your home to be?
5. How many children will you have? When do you want to have them? Will you use birth control?
6. How will you raise your children? What kind of school will they go to?
7. Do you like children?
8. How do you want to use your leisure time? What hobbies do you have?
9. What kind of food do you like?
10. Are you affectionate?
11. What are your sexual expectations?
12. Do you agree about religion?
13. Do you agree about politics?
14. How will you handle conflicts with relatives?
15. Will you have a boys/girls night out?
16. What pets will you have?
17. Is it ok for your spouse to have an opposite sexed friend?
18. What do you like for music, television and movies?
19. How can you improve communication?
20. How can you resolve conflict better?
21. Where do you want to live?
22. What are you financial goals? It is recommended you write a budget together.
23. Whose family will you spend holidays with?
24. Will the wife take the husband's last name?
25. When will you marry?
26. Where will you marry?
27. How much will spend on your wedding?
28. What will the vows be?
29. Where will you go on a honeymoon?
30. Will either spouse continue education after the wedding?
31. Will you maintain your appearance after the wedding?
32. Will you seek counseling if there's a serious problem?
33. What adult baggage do you have?
34. What do you like about the other?
35. What would you like to change about the other?
36. What do you want form each other?

THINGS TO DO ON DATES

1. Go to dinner, lunch or Sunday brunch.
2. Attend a movie, play or concert.
3. Go on a picnic.
4. Go swimming, boating or water skiing.
5. Go to a circus or carnival.
6. Go hiking.
7. Go shopping.
8. Take a fun class together.
9. Visit friends or relatives.
10. Go to church.
11. Cook together.
12. Surf the internet.
13. Take a drive in the countryside.
14. Go snow skiing.
15. Make arts and crafts.
16. Play board games.
17. Play music, listen to music or sing karaoke.
18. Use a batting cage.
19. Bowl.
20. Golf.
21. Ride bicycles.
22. Bird watch.
23. Dance.
24. Read a book together.
25. Write a song together.
26. Go to a comedy club.
27. Visit a museum.
28. Exercise together.
29. Volunteer together.
30. Attend a parade.
31. Star gaze.
32. Attend a sports event.
33. Ice skate.
34. Visit an indoor climbing gym.
35. Attend a mystery murder diner.
36. Site see.
37. Exercise together.
38. Attend a wine tasting.

Reasonable self-advocacy is important for Aspies. Like some members of some other groups they face discrimination. Discrimination is a poison that ruins lives. They need to stand up for their rights or they will be stepped on.   At the same time they need make a good impression and not blame all of their failures on discrimination. Everyone judges everyone else. Judgment doesn't occur in a vacuum. If someone is an Aspie he will be judged in part on what people already think about Aspies and in part on himself. How people judge someone has a lot to do with determining how good his life will be. Life isn't fair.

As a member of a group that is commonly discriminated against, an Aspie should be aware of his legal rights. Federal, state and local laws and regulations provide some protection. An Aspie should know where to make a complaint. Making a complaint is greatly helped by keeping a careful written record of what happened noting who else was present and save a copy of all written communication.

Negative stereotypes need to be broken.   A stereotype is a preconception of what a group of people are like. It's used to prejudge people and it can be changed. Aspies would benefit greatly from changing the stereotype others have of them. Looking good and speaking well are important. So is being friendly. Aspies are notorious for not liking physical activity so one thing they could do is train and take part in athletic competitions. Some people think Aspies are lacking in empathy so it would help for them to volunteer.   It would also help for Aspies to take an interest in those topics of interest to others. Needless to say it would also help to make some friends.

Not ever failure is the result of discrimination. Not getting a job is a good example. Maybe someone more qualified applied. When hiring it's important not just to hire the most qualified person but someone who fits in with the culture of the organization. Each organization has its own culture and someone who doesn't fit in would be disruptive. A radical environmental organization wouldn't likely hire someone conservative. A conservative think tank might feel uncomfortable with a progressive.

FAMOUS PEOPLE THOUGHT OT HAVE ASPERGER'S

Bill Gates	Businessman
Alfred Hitchcook	Movie Director
Isaac Newton	Scientist
Jane Austen	Writer
Wolfgang Mozart	Composer
Ludwig Van Bethoven	Composer
Henry Ford	Industrialist
Albert Einstein	Scientist
Vincent Van Gough	Artist
Daryl Hannah	Actress
Bob Dylan	Singer
Andy Warhol	Artist
Nikola Telsa	Scientist
Mark Twain	Writer
Julian Assange	Journalist
Charles Darwin	Scientist
Marie Curie	Scientist
Gregor Mendel	Scientist
Carl Sagan	Scientist
John Watson	Psychologist
Lewis Carroll	Writer
Abraham Lincoln	President of US
Howard Hughes	Businessman

PHYSICAL DEVELOPMENT

Young adulthood provides an athletic opportunity. Physical development is a problem for Aspie men. They grow up being bullied. Every child is bullied, but Aspie children are bullied much more than others. As a result they develop a sense of fear and carry bad memories. They often have physical problems when they are children, but partially overcome them as they become adults. Most don't play sports in school and they're not happy about their bodies. They often become more athletic in young adulthood. Typically they become weightlifters or martial artists. Weightlifters typically work out three nonconsecutive days a week. Weightlifting and aerobics are done each workout. Martial arts can be an alternative. There are many to choose from. The best one depends on the build of the student and usually takes two or three nights a week to learn. It's possible to combine weightlifting and martial arts, but it's not typically done because most martial arts instructors think weightlifting reduces quickness and flexibility. Martial artists run, stretch and do calisthenics. *Added strength or skill provides confidence and increases self-esteem.* Physical development is a problem for Aspie women too. They often feel unattractive. Swimming is a common choice of Aspie women and jogging could also be good. *Women gain self-esteem and confidence with improved appearance.* Finding dates becomes much easier. Swimming or jogging requires working out three nonconsecutive days a week. A small number of Aspies have become professional athletes. It's possible because not all Aspies are physically affected. An Aspie who isn't physically affected should have the same chance to become an athlete as anyone else.

Sherwood, S. (2012). 10 Ways Men and Women Communicate Differently. Retrieved from
http://dsc.discovery.comtv-shows/curiosity/topic/ways-men-and-women-cmunnimcate-differently.

HOW PARENTS CAN HELP

PARENTS CAN TAKE SOME RESPONSIBILITY

How should parents react? When parents hear Asperger's Syndrome they ask, "What is that". The word Autism hits like a bomb. *It's natural that parents are concerned, but it's important they not panic.* Panicking never helps anyone. Asperger's Syndrome isn't a death sentence. Parents need a plan. The plan should address education, advocacy, normalcy, therapy and talents. There is a great need for education. Parents need to educate themselves, teachers need to do the same and parents need to educate children. It's important that parents advocate for their children, especially those who have special needs, so they get the help they require. . Parents should teach their children to be as normal as possible, so they will fit in better with other children. Children with A.S. often need therapy of some kind, if not because of A.S. then because of associated disorders. A special talent is a possible benefit from A.S. and parents should try to identify special talents and encourage their children to develop them. They should also teach social skills.

Education is the key. Parents should begin by educating themselves. They can't rely on doctors to tell them what they need to know. It's important for them to read lots of books about A.S. Joining a parent support group is a good idea. So is talking to a psychologist. When reading about A.S. parents should take careful notes that they can easily refer to in the future. They should also come up with a list of questions to ask experts. Educating teachers I also critical because children spend so much time at school and A.S. affects learning. Not all teachers are familiar with A.S. Parents should meet with teachers at the beginning of each school year to make sure teachers know their child has A.S. and knows what they can do to help. Telling a child he has A.S. can be difficult. Children need to know and have a right to know at some point. It might be appropriate to talk about it during the summer between grade school and middle school. *The summer might be a good time because if a child has problems dealing with it he will have the summer to adjust before going back to school.* Children at that age can handle some situations, but parents should talk about how normal they are and point out that lots of other children also have problems. The child should be given basic information about A.S. Not telling could cause more problems latter as a child will eventually find out and might feel bitter about not having been told.

A child with A.S. will have more difficulty than other children. That is to be expected. *Parents and teachers should work together, but at time parents need to be advocates.* Advocating is needed to make sure their children get the help they need and that teachers show kindness and patience. If parents are going to advocate they need to know what is going on in the life of their child and that requires communication. Parents should speak with a child every school day about what happened at school. They should also communicate with teachers often. A good way to do that in the early grades is with a notebook the child carries between home and school. Frequent communication show teachers that parents care and it helps build rapport which can be critical when advocating.

TEACHING NORMALCY IS IMPORTANT

Normalcy training is the big challenge facing parents. ***Children with A.S. aren't normal, but they should be raised to be a normal as they reasonably can be.*** That means they must be able to use nonverbal communication, understand figurative language, dress appropriately, understand the feelings of others and have close to normal interests. They can be taught to be almost normal, but patience is needed because they are being asked to do some things that aren't normal for them.

Effectively using nonverbal communication is critical. People communicate almost as much with nonverbal communication as they do with verbal communication. Body language, facial expression, personal space and tone of voice are important. Role play and drawing can be helpful. A parent could draw several images of people using body language and the child could copy those drawings. Afterwards parents could model body language and then the child could do the same. In those ways the child could learn to recognize the meaning of body language when used by others and learn to use body language himself. The same could be done to teach the use of facial expressions. Personal space is the distance between people and it varies from nation to nation and situation to situation. Children need to be taught to maintain proper physical distance. They should know when it's appropriate to touch and when it isn't. Tone of voice and be important. Most children know when their parents and teachers are really angry with them by tone of voice. A child with A.S. could have trouble doing that. He should be taught how to understand tone of voice and how to use it.

A child needs to learn to empathize with others to get along. ***Empathy often develops naturally, but for children with A.S. some training might be needed.*** Role lay is a good way to learn empathy. Have the child role play different empathy provoking situations and describe how he feels when playing each part and also have him talk about what he could do to help another child who feels that way. In that way empathy can be learned with practice.

Clothing chose is important for those with A.S. They often dress strangely because they have a desire for sameness and they are tactile sensitive. If left to themselves they might wear the same clothes ever. They need to learn what others consider acceptable attire. ***A rotation schedule is a good idea.*** Perhaps there can be some sameness by buying similar clothes of different colors. Tactile sensitivity leads those with A.S. to wear soft shirts and no t-shirts. That might not be a problem in some situations. Children with A.S. will be happier wearing soft clothes.

What to do about a special interest is always an issue. A typical child with A.S. has a topic of special interest and spends all of his available learning about it to the exclusion of everything else. The interest could be in anything and it might change over time. There's nothing wrong with having a special interest, but it's a problem if it crowds out normal interests. ***Maybe it would be best not to discourage a special interest but to encourage other interests that are age appropriate.*** For example, a child might be obsessed about space travel or dinosaurs. Discouraging that makes little sense but maybe it would be a good idea to encourage an interest in baseball, scouts, music or sports.

THERAPY

A child with A.S. will need therapy. Each child is different and a child might need therapy at some times more than others. One child with A.S. might develop several associated disorders and another might never have any. Parents should be on the lookout for associated disorders. ***They should look for attention deficit disorder, hyperactivity disorder, speech problems and clumsiness when a child is small and almost expect problems with anxiety and depression when the child reaches puberty***. Tourette's and bipolar disorder are less common, but they should be watched for. Teachers and doctors can help keep watch for problems. Schools can provide some therapy.

Explaining therapy to a child can be difficult because a young person might not understand. A child might ask why he needs therapy when other children don't. He might wonder what's wrong with him. ***Parents should stress how normal he is and talk about therapy other children get***. It would also be helpful to assure him that therapy won't be needed forever. The goal of therapy should be clearly explained.

TALENTS ARE IMPORTANT

A parent should help a child identify and develop talents. The most common talents are mathematics, music, foreign languages, art, acting, writing, computer programming, engineering visualization, calendar skills and chess. Identifying talents requires trying a variety of activities. A child who never tries music will never learn if he has a musical talent. The same is true of all talents. Parents should encourage children to try many things and take notice of how well they do to identify talents. Children often become too interested in only one thing, often playing soccer. Playing soccer is fine, but lots of scientists and musicians went undiscovered because all they did was play soccer. The summer is a good time for parents to look for talents in their children because that's when children have time. Perhaps a different talent could be looked for each summer. Parents shouldn't be surprised if their child doesn't have a special talent because lots of children with A.S. don't. If nothing else it will keep children busy and hopefully they will enjoy it. Once a talent is identified it needs to be developed. That requires time and work.

Mathematical talent is the most important because it's the foundation of science. *A child with great mathematical ability and intense focus might have what it takes to become successful in medicine, dentistry, engineering or science.* Providing lots of extra math instruction during summer vacations is a good idea. There is a problem. A student might become more advanced than classmates and feel bored with mathematics during school. Parents should talk with teachers about more advanced mathematics courses.

Developing musical talent takes work. An Aspie child without a monotone voice might be able to learn to sing. Most Aspie children will never learn to sing because they lack range. Learning to play an instrument is much more likely. It includes learning to read music. Some schools offer good music programs including chorus, a marching band and maybe even a symphony. Lots of others don't. Private lessons might be possible. It's not possible to learn to play classical music well without instruction but children might be able to learn other kinds of music with a little help from parents. Start with listening to music. The plan should be to learn one instrument at a time. It could be a good idea to start learning with bongos to keep time. Possible good combination might include piano and guitar, banjo and guitar, violin and mandolin, flute and clarinet and bass and drums.

Learning multiple foreign languages is a real possibility. It requires work can be interesting and very useful. Learning the first one is the most difficult. Learning subsequent similar languages is much easier. French, Spanish, Italian, Portuguese and Romanian are similar. German, Dutch, Swedish and Norwegian are similar. So are Russian, Polish, Ukrainian and Czech. Chinese, Japanese and Hindi are possible but more difficult. There is a dispute about when a child should begin to learn a foreign language. Some people say at age three and others at age eleven. Eleven is common because that's when some schools start offering foreign language classes. Early exposure to foreign language songs might be a good idea. Learning a foreign language includes learning a foreign culture. For example, one must understand the French to use French effectively.

Art is an excellent talent. There was never a time when art didn't help to shape culture. **A great way to begin is with a trip to an art museum.** Another is watching a video about an artist working. Some schools have good art programs, but most don't. Learning to make art should start with describing objects. Making objects out of paper should follow. Next comes drawing them. At that point it's a good idea to do some simple painting. Next should making simple objects out of clay. After that it's time to learn about art history and make more complex art.

Acting is fun but requires work. Begin with watching television and movies and attending a play. Next it's time for role play. **Have the child role play lots parts he is familiar with from television shows.** There are some schools that offer opportunities to participate in plays, but lots more don't. Look for opportunities for children to participate in local community theater.

Parents can help a child develop a talent for creative writing. Take the child to a library to get some books. **When he can read simple books to his parents he's ready to write simple creative story.** Begin by having the child tell a made up story and then write it down. Have the child work on developing characters, then describing action and finally on plot development. Some schools and libraries offer creative writing competitions.

Computer programming is an important talent that a child can develop. The internet will become only more important in the future and students will one day use computers at school in the same way their parents used books. **Children who can't use computers will be left behind.** Lots of schools teach students to use computers, but it helps to have one at home to practice on. Programming is what makes computers work. It's possible to use a computer reasonably well without knowing how to write programs, but being able to write programs makes it possible to use computers even more effectively. A computer program looks like lines of code, because that's what it is. A program is lines of code that give instructions to computers. That code is translated into machine language which computers can understand. The basic language is the simplest so it's the one people learn first. A child could learn to write a simple program using basic. After that he could write more complex programs in Basic and eventually learn other computer languages. It would be best to start with a very simple book on Basic.

Some children with A.S. have the remarkable talent of visualizing for engineering. **Someone with that talent can accurately imagine what parts in a machine look like from different vantage points and how they work.** An excellent way to develop that talent might be to take simple safe machines apart and then draw all of the parts showing how they fit together. Next might be to draw how the machines what the machines would look like from various vantage points. Lastly it could be constructing simple machines from wood, glue, tape, staples, paper and clay. A child might eventually be able to construct a real working machine. Safety comes first of course. A few high schools offer classes in machine shop, auto shop and drafting which could help greatly. The visualization talent combines with the mathematical talent and intense focus would provide the makings for a very good engineer. The visualization talent could also reinforce the art talent. It could be the basis of a career in drafting on its own.

Chess is a talent. A child with A.S. should be encouraged to play. Some schools have chess teams. It's important to learn chess from a book to know the standard moves.

SOCIAL SKILLS

Parents should teach social skills. Children with A.S. have lots of trouble interacting with other children because they don't understand how to interact. Most children quickly pick up on rules of interaction, but those with A.S. need extra instruction. ***They need to learn politeness and friendship.***

Politeness requires learning rules. A child must learn to speak appropriately. That means using appropriate language and talking in turn. Those with A.S. might have great difficulty understanding when others have stopped talking so they can talk. They could have difficulty understanding the need to avoid offending people. ***Role paly can help teach politeness.***

Learning to be a friend is critical for children with A.S. Everyone needs friends and children with A.S. have a lot of trouble doing that. Part of the reason is they seem odd. Perhaps a bigger part is they have difficulty learning to be friends. It would help greatly if parents would teach a child to be loyal to friends, to show interest in what their friends like and to be willing to help others. It would also be helpful for parents to encourage their children to take part in social activities. ***Children with A.S. normally avoid social activities because they fear rejection, but if they avoid those activities they won't make friends.***

HOW TEACHERS CAN HELP

AN OPPORTUNITY TO BECOME A BETTER TEACHER

A teacher is told she has a child with Asperger's Syndrome in her class. His first thought might be what's expected of me know. He might never had a student with Asperger's Syndrome and not know anything about it. The best way to approach the challenge is to see it as an opportunity for professional development. *He will need to learn about the disorder, teach creatively, provide a friendly environment, facilitate social development and protect.*

A teacher is a learner. Continuing to learn is part of the definition of professionalism. *A teacher needs to learn about the problems his students have.* That includes Asperger's Syndrome. Reading a book about it is the place to start. After compiling a list of questions speaking to other teachers and the parents of the child is a good idea. Each child is unique so the teacher should keep an open mind. Children change fast as they grow so a child could be very different at the end of a school year from what he was like in the beginning.

Lots of students with A.S. might also have been diagnosed N.L.D. Symptoms includes an impaired ability to see the big picture, trouble with visual spatial perception, poor appreciation of body in space and possibly left side neglect. It also includes poor motor coordination, mostly on the left side and weak reading comprehension and spelling skills, poor conceptual math skills and impaired organization skills. (Smart Kids, n.d.) *The effects are pervasive because there are several symptoms.* Each needs to be considered individually.

A big part of the problem is difficulty using language. Spelling can be improved with extra practice. The difficulty with spelling might be phonetic use of language. Lots of words in English are pronounced differently than they are spelled. Students with N.L.D. might naturally spell words the way the sound. Learning to pronounce them correctly is critical, but perhaps students can also learn to mispronounce them so they can be spelled correctly. Reading comprehension might be improved by having students draw sketches showing what happened in a story. Learning a foreign language can be a big challenge for someone with N.L.V.D. Sketching the plots of foreign language stories could be beneficial. It might also help to diagram dialogue. They could be helped by role playing a dialogue from each point of view. Foreign words might be more difficult to spell than words in English.

Math comprehension is another problem. It shows up with word problems, algebra, geometry, trigonometry and calculus. That's because it's difficult for students with N.L.D. to understand what those kind of math problems are asking. One possible solution might be to explain to students what those problems are asking, and latter have them explain that they are asking before attempting to solve them. It could also be helpful to diagram them. Students can't answer math problems if they don't know what they are asking. Math seems mysterious to them and they just don't get it. Not understanding could end what could have become many promising careers.

School can be a good or bad experience for students with N.L.D. It will be a bad experience if their different needs are not considered. A student with N.L.D. might not be able to look a teacher in the eye or possibly even the face. The student might look away from the teacher when listening and might not understand some of the words he uses or repeat questions. It's also possible the student might not be respectful of personal space boundaries. A teacher should always stand to the right of a student with N.L.V.D. Teachers are responsible for helping students to socially develop and that includes making friends. A teacher must also be a protector. Students with N.L.D. commonly have problems with being bullied. Teachers need to prevent bullying to the extent they are able.

Communicate with N.L.D. students appropriately. Stand to the right and speak in a clam voice. Don't use big words because the student might not understand them, even if he uses them. Don't worry if the student doesn't make eye contact or even looks away. If a student repeats a question or comment, possibly over and over realize it might be because the thought is stuck in his brain. It might be required to teach a student to use appropriate personal space.

Like others with Autism those with A.S. requires a great deal of sameness. They do best with structure. It's important for them to do the same things at the same times each day. If a school schedule is going to be different it's a good idea to let them know ahead of time and to explain why. They also need to interact with the same people. If there will be a substitute teacher it would be a good idea to let them know beforehand. In general transitions should be minimized.

Making friends is daunting challenge for students with A.S. so they need help. No one wants to grow up without any friends. Students with A.S. are typically socially rejected because they are different. Normal children don't like children who have problems. A teacher could help a student with A.S. to make friends by assigning group work so that student has opportunities to interact with other students.

A teacher should keep the secret. Lots of children with A.S. don't know they have it. They need to be told when they are ready, but a teacher shouldn't tell a student he has a problem before parents are ready for him to know.

Bullying is a big problem. Adults with A.S. often say bullying was the biggest problem they had. Logically that's most true for those who are smaller and weaker. *Every school should have a no bullying policy.* Bullies should face discipline and teachers should talk about the policy with students. Teachers need to be aware that a lot of bullying occurs while travelling to and from school and online.

Smart Kids. (n.d.). Retrieved From http://www.smartkidswithld.org/ld...symptoms/signs-symptoms-of-ld.

MARRIAGE AND ASPERGER'S SYNDROME

UNDERSTAND HOW ASPERGER'S SYNDROME AFFECTS MARRIAGE

Marriage to someone with A.S. is a challenge. Lots of people with A.S. have difficulty feeling loved. That makes emotional commitment more difficult for them. All couples have communication problems which is also difficult for those with A.S. They might have special interests and not understand social rules. A desire for sameness and rigid thinking could be problems. Sex could also be an issue.

Bonding, communication and special interests could be issues. Everyone wants to be in love and be loved. Someone with A.S. might have trouble feeling loved. *That could make bonding more difficult.* Weak bonding might increase the risk of divorce. Men and women have trouble communicating. *A lot of important couple communication happens nonverbally.* That is a big problem for a spouse with A.S. Someone with A.S. can learn to use nonverbal communication. A person with A.S. likely has a special interest. *That could drive a spouse crazy.* Maybe there could be a rule about not discussing it at home.

Not understanding social rules could be a critical problem. For example, someone with A.S. might consider any negative comments, even constructive criticism of self, relatives or friends as a personal attack. *Another problem might be a spouse with A.S. violating social rules inadvertently because he doesn't understand them.* He could say or do something that offends someone.

Sameness and rigidity could be issues. Someone with a strong desire for sameness might resist even small changes in routine. For example, he might want to get up and go to bed at the same time every day and eat the same food according to a schedule. Rigid thinking could make accepting new ideas very difficult.

Sex is a critical issue because marriage won't survive without it. Anecdotal evidence points to diminished sexual desire among men with A.S. *That might not be so bad because sexual desire can be increased.* One key is not smoking. Smoking reduces sexual desire. (Sex and Smoking, 2008) Another is to do aerobic exercise. Aerobic exercise increases sexual desire. (Improve Your Sex Life, 2010) It might also help to be well rested, make time for sex and set the mood. As a result of the desire for sameness someone with A.S. might want to have sex on the same days and at the same times. An understanding spouse would help greatly.

Healing begins with a diagnosis. Before there is a diagnosis misunderstandings and fear abound. After a diagnosis is accepted a couple can start to move forward. Understanding and counseling can begin. *A diagnosis isn't a cure; it's the first step in learning to live with the disorder.*

Marriage enhancement should focus on building up specific skills. *Recognizing emotions, using nonverbal communication, feeling empathy and communicating effectively are the most important.* Together they can make a huge difference for couples.

It's important for people with A.S. to learn how to recognize emotions because they are as important determiners human behavior as much as logic does. Emotions often overwhelm logic and that can lead to critical relationship situations. That's certainly true when anger or jealousy are involved. People with A.S. have trouble understanding the emotions others feel because emotions are usually communicated by facial expressions, body language, tone of voice and personal space. Those with A.S. have difficulty picking up on those kinds of communication. Golan, O., Ashwin, E., Granader, Y., McClintock, S., Kay, K. and Leggett, V. & Baron-Cohen, S. (2010) used an interactive DVD to increase emotional recognition in children with A.S. No doubt adults with A.S. could be taught to recognize the emotions of spouses which would greatly aid communication. Failure to recognize emotions should be seen as a training problem.

Role play could be very useful reinforcing the learning of body language and empathy. Someone with A.S. could be taught to communicate nonverbally with practice. He could also learn to understand others nonverbal communication. The best way to do that would be for the person to practice expressing emotions and also guessing emotions that others express. By playing the role of others in distressing situations those with A.S. can learn to be empathic.

Effective communication depends on rules. Important rules are to avoid personal attacks, stick to the issue, don't threaten, speak calmly and discuss issues only at the appropriate times. It's essential to seek win-win solutions so no one feels taken advantage of. Everyone should remember conflict isn't about power; it's about solving problems together.

Golan, O., Ashwin, E., Granader, Y., McClintock, S., Kay, K. and Leggett, V. & Baron-Cohen, S. (2010). Enhancing emotion recognition in children with autism spectrum conditions: an intervention using animated vehicles with real emotional faces. *Journal of autism and developmental disorders* 40(3): 269-279.

Improve your Sex Life. (2010). Retrieved From http://www.thelifeco.com/improve-your-sex-life-with-exercise.

Sex and Smoking. (2008). Retrieved From http://www.ecigarettedirect.co.uk/articles/smoking-sex.